# WINNING THE
# INVESTMENT
# GAME

# WINNING THE INVESTMENT GAME

## A GUIDE FOR ALL SEASONS

JAMES H. GIPSON

McGraw-Hill Book Company

New York   St. Louis   San Francisco   Auckland   Bogotá   Hamburg   Johannesburg
London   Madrid   Mexico   Montreal   New Delhi   Panama   Paris   São Paulo
Singapore   Sydney   Tokyo   Toronto

For my wife and for my mother

Library of Congress Cataloging in Publication Data
Gipson, James H.
Winning the investment game.
Includes index.
1. Investments—Handbooks, manuals, etc.  I. Title.
HG4527.G56      1984        332.6'78       83-17540
ISBN 0-07-023292-X

1234567890 DOCDOC 8987654

ISBN 0-07-023292-X

The editors for this book were William A. Sabin and William B. O'Neal, the designer was Dennis Sharkey, and the production supervisor was Reiko F. Okamura. It was set in Caledonia by Datagraphics.

Printed and bound by R. R. Donnelley & Sons Company

# CONTENTS

# TEN.    THE VIRTUES OF INVESTING    151

# APPENDIX.    MODERN PORTFOLIO THEORY    166

# PREFACE

This is a book about making money, keeping it, and having fun in the process.

The ideas presented here are intended to be enduring ones rather than a trendy explanation of current events which is outdated by the time it is published. The reader who picks up this book a decade from now will find some of the examples out of date, but will find the investment strategies still useful. Investing, unlike physics, is one business where there is seldom anything really new under the sun. There are a few basic principles and strategies for investors to learn; they can then spend the remainder of their investing careers applying them.

None of the ideas presented here is particularly difficult to grasp. The difficulty lies less in understanding the new ideas than in abandoning the old ones which are less useful. Successful investing requires a different mode of thinking and acting than most other activities do. Dressing fashionably is a sensible way to go through life with a minimum of social problems, but investing fashionably is a near guarantee of profit problems. A contrary, independent attitude is essential, as is a recognition of why investment trends end and how to avoid losing money when they do.

Professional investors may find this book useful in integrating economics and investing. An enormous amount of human energy and computer power is expended by institutional investors on forecasting the economy with the seldom realized hope that superior forecasts will translate into superior profits. An alternative to the conventional approach is offered which is likely to prove a better way to turn economic knowledge into financial profit.

While professional investors may benefit from the ideas in this book, professional jargon is kept to a minimum. Most things in life really worth knowing can be expressed in lucid sentences of the English language rather than in jargon whose purpose is to make the profession obscure and therefore impressive to outsiders. Any investor who can understand *The Wall Street Journal* or the business section of a local paper should have no difficulty.

Another note on language: There exists no neuter personal pronoun in English meaning "he or she," and by convention such words as "he" and "his" and "himself" are used as indefinite pronouns, referring generically to both sexes. The alternatives to this grammatical imprecision, such as actually writing "he or she" and "her or his," upon repeated use, often make the language stilted and unwieldy—the cure becomes worse than the disease. In the interest of brevity, the generic *he, his,* and so on are adopted in this book, with the intent that in general cases such pronouns be understood to refer to a person of either sex.

Investing is a serious business, but that does not mean that investors need take themselves seriously too. The investing game can be viewed as an intellectual challenge in competition with some of the best and most aggressive minds in the country. No one wins all the time, but an investor who wins more often than most can find the investing game as enjoyable as it is profitable.

James H. Gipson

# ABOUT
# THE AUTHOR

James Gipson is president of Pacific Financial Research. He received his M.B.A. from Harvard Business School and has been an investment manager for mutual funds and institutional clients for the last 10 years. Before that he was a management consultant with McKinsey & Company.

Many of his articles have appeared in the *Washington Post*. He has also published articles in the *Boston Globe, Journal of Portfolio Management,* and *Pensions and Investments Age.*

# CHAPTER ONE

# THE NAMES OF THE GAMES

Making money and keeping it is the payoff from playing the investment game well. As in tennis or golf, winning in the investing game requires the players to recognize what game is being played, learn its rules, and then practice until they are more proficient than their opponents.

Recognizing what game is being played is easier said than done. The basic idea of this book is that there are three distinct investment games, each of which may last for as long as a generation. Each game sows the seeds of its own destruction, and then another game begins. The largest profits belong to investors who correctly recognize the current game (most investors, like French generals, are too busy fighting the last war to win the current one) and play it well. The worst losses accrue to investors who fail to recognize the name of the current game or fail to recognize when games change.

This chapter summarizes the theory of the three basic investment games and suggests which assets do best and worst in each of them. Chapters 2 to 8 deal with the past and summarize how investors prospered and perished in the last three games from 1929 to 1980. Chapter 9 deals with the future and offers the author's ideas as to where we go from here. Chapter 10 explains the virtues of investing where virtue is more than its own reward.

# THE THEORY OF THE THREE GAMES IN A NUTSHELL

Investment assets are like fruits which mature in different seasons. No single asset is good during all seasons, but each one can be very profitable at the right time. The three major investment games determine the right season for each of the major assets available to investors: stocks, bonds, cash, real estate, gold, and tangible assets such as coins, stamps, antiques, and art.

The positive sum game is the the best of all possible worlds. Growth is good and more growth is better. Common stocks do very well, particularly if those stocks are in companies enjoying rapid real growth in goods or services they produce. Real estate does well if located in a growth market. Cash, bonds, and tangible assets are likely to be losers both in real terms and in comparison with better opportunities available elsewhere. The golden age of growth and the positive sum investing game was 1950 to 1973.

The zero sum investing game is like poker where there is a loser for every winner. New wealth is not created by working hard, saving frugally, and investing intelligently. Instead, existing wealth is shifted around the table in favor of clever players who capitalize on inflation. Real estate, gold, and tangibles all do very well as investors rush from a rotting dollar into assets which they hope will preserve the real value of their capital. A few common stocks do well if they are in exceptional companies which capitalize on inflation, but most stocks lose value in real terms. Cash equivalents such as Treasury bills are losers in real terms, and bonds are a prescription for financial euthanasia. The inflation which took off in 1973 began the zero sum investing game of the 1970s.

The negative sum investing game is the worst of all possible worlds. As the real wealth of society contracts in a long depression, most investors lose money in tangible assets and in gold. Real estate and stocks are also losers unless their rents and profits are very stable. Cash equivalents and bonds, which produced nothing but real and opportunity losses during the previous two games, emerge as unexpected winners. The depression of the 1930s was the last major negative sum investing game.

# ECONOMICS AND INVESTING— THE ECONOMY CALLS THE GAME

Common sense rightly suggests that the economy has a powerful influence on investing success. Common sense, unfortunately, does not suggest precisely what that influence is. The conventional approach (next section) tries and usually fails to use short-term forecasts of the economy as the basis of intelligent investment decisions. A less conventional but more straightforward approach is to use the long-term state of the economy to indicate which investing game to play.

The dominant trend in the economy determines which investing game is profitable to play. The three investing games are merely reflections of the long-run trend of the economy: positive sum, zero sum, and negative sum.

The creation of real wealth is the dominant trend of a positive sum economy. Growth of the labor force, improvements in education, advances in technology, and investment in capital goods combine to multiply the real wealth available to society. Prices remain stable or rise only moderately in relation to the gains in real GNP. The way to capitalize on this creation of real wealth is to invest in the stocks of companies which create that growth and in real estate which benefits from it. The 1950–1973 period was the last great positive sum economy.

The transfer of real wealth, not its creation, is the dominant trend of a zero sum economy such as the United States experienced in the late 1970s. As real economic growth slows down and inflation heats up, the energy of intelligent men and women shifts from working to enlarge the nation's economic pie to fighting for an enlarged piece of it. Inflation is the peaceful means by which wealth and income are transferred from inept players to adept ones; revolution is the traditionally less peaceful means. The major opportunities available to investors are the beneficiaries of inflation: gold, real estate, and tangible assets.

The destruction of real wealth is the dominant trend of a negative sum economy. Depressions are nasty events, but they are the only sure cure for inflation. A depression is most dangerous when it slips beyond the ability of government to control it or when it is compounded by the well-intentioned blunders of people in power. Caught in a shrinking economy, most investors see the real value of their assets shrink too. The few investors who increase the real value of their assets are ones who play the negative sum investing game.

## ECONOMICS AND INVESTING— WHY THE CONVENTIONAL APPROACH DOES NOT WORK

Money may be managed profitably or conventionally, but not both. A recurring theme of this book is the need for an investor to take a contrary, unconventional approach toward investing. The failure of the conventional approach of relating economics to investing is one example of the need for contrary, unconventional thinking.

The conventional approach uses a short-term economic forecast as the basis for predicting stock prices. If a recession is predicted, then stocks are sold now in the expectation that they will decline along with the earnings of the companies they represent. If capital spending is expected to be strong next year, then stocks of capital goods producers are purchased now. This conventional approach has a great deal of intuitive appeal and only one drawback—it does not work in producing superior investment returns.

The problem with the conventional approach is that the stock market anticipates the economy rather than the other way around. The Commerce Department uses 12 leading indicators to forecast the economy's direction, and the stock market is one of the best of those leading indicators. By the time a recession is apparent, the stock market generally has declined already. The stock market generally hits bottom about 6 months before the economy does and it rises long before recovery is apparent. The bear market of 1973 to 1974 was a prime example: the stock market peaked nearly 1 year before the recession began in the fall of 1973 and then bottomed in the fall of 1974, 6 months before the economy began to recover.

The stock market represents the consensus of millions of well-informed investors (and millions of badly informed investors too). By the time an investor recognizes that some major economic change is under way, it is probably old news to millions of other investors. *The price of stocks today reflects the consensus of investors' expectations about the future, so investors are unlikely to make money unless their expectations about the future are both correct and significantly different from the consensus.*

An individual investor who employs the conventional approach of using economic forecasts to predict stock prices is at a significant disadvantage to institutional investors with far greater resources at their disposal. Bank trust departments, insurance companies, and large investment counselors use a great deal of brainpower and computer power to make highly detailed short-term forecasts of the economy; they are far more likely to spot changing economic patterns than an individual investor is.

Many individual investors feel intimidated when they realize they are competing against the vast human and computer resources of institutional investors. They shouldn't. True, institutional investors have competent economists who work long and hard to produce forecasts which are not available to individual investors. Also true, however, is that many of those forecasts are dead wrong. In late 1973 most economists predicted a "soft landing" for the economy in the following year, not the worst recession in 40 years which actually occurred. In the 8 quarters of 1980 through 1981, the consensus of economists was wrong an amazing six times about whether real GNP would go up or down over the next 3 months.

Institutional investors often are wrong in their economic predictions, but they still stand a better chance of being right than the average individual investor. Being right, however, is usually not very helpful. Like other human beings confronted by an uncertain future and by unpleasant consequences for being wrong about the future, most economists huddle together for safety and thereby produce broadly similar economic forecasts. Most economists use similar economic models and common sources of data such as those provided by the government and Data Resources, Inc., so it is hardly surprising that their forecasts resemble each other closely. Each forecast generally contains a few small differences from the consensus to show that the forecaster has done some work, but those differences are seldom enough to produce superior performance.

The bottom line of superior performance is where the conventional approach really breaks down. Long-term studies of performance by monitoring firms such as A. G. Becker indicate that up to 80 percent of institutional investors *under*perform the market over 5-, 10-, and 15-year periods. Most institutional investors do well once in a while (a phenomenon known in the business as "every dog has its day"), but there is depressingly little evidence to show that institutions really deliver superior returns. So much evidence about the mediocrity of institutional investors accumulated in the late 1960s and early 1970s that the random walk theory (also known as the efficient market hypothesis) was born, a subject covered in greater detail in the Appendix.

## THE END OF AN INVESTING GAME

No game lasts forever. Merely recognizing that fact gives an investor a major advantage over most other investors who project the trends of the immediate past into the indefinite future. Any single game may last as long as a generation, but eventually it sows the seeds of its own destruction and another game emerges. The end of a game is a messy affair which creates a crisis for investors.

A crisis is not all bad. The Chinese recognized that fact when they created the symbol for the word "crisis" by combining the symbols for two other words: danger and opportunity. A major element of success-ful investing is avoiding the dangers presented by a new game while capitalizing on its opportunities.

The dangers are always more apparent in retrospect than in the euphoria which accompanies the end of a game. Few investors in the excitement of 1929 realized how badly stocks would perform during the negative sum investing game of the 1930s. More recently, few investors in the roaring bull market of the late 1960s realized how badly stocks and bonds would perform during the zero sum investing game of the 1970s. Even more recently, many investors in 1979 believed that real estate prices only go up, a belief which was very hazardous to their financial health.

The other side of danger is opportunity. The negative sum investing game of the 1930s created a great opportunity for holders of cash and bonds to increase the real value of their capital. A similar opportunity existed for gold, real estate, and other tangible assets during the zero sum investing game of the 1970s. Opportunity is present in every game, particularly in times of greatest crisis. One of the early Rothschilds observed that the time to buy is when blood is running in the streets; a modern version of that observation is that opportunity is at its maxi-mum when investors are just plain scared.

Danger and opportunity are the two constants of investing. They are always present, but are not always apparent. Only the opportunity to jump on the bandwagon was apparent to most stockholders in 1969 and to most property owners in 1979, but danger was at its greatest point for both groups of investors then. Because the end of an investing game creates a whole new set of dangers and opportunities and because recognizing them is so critical to investment success, each of the three following chapters on the three games has a separate section on how to recognize the current game and how to tell when it changes.

## WHY GAMES END—THE LOGIC OF INVESTING

Once a game goes on for a decade or more, there is a temptation to think it will last forever. The reason why no game lasts forever goes to the heart of an often unquestioned assumption about the form of logic investors should use.

Most investors use linear logic, a method taught in science courses to every high school student. If water boils at 100°C in 1000 straight experiments, then the odds are very good that it will boil at that same temperature on the next try. If the sun has risen in the east every morning since the dawn of history, then one may conclude that it will rise from that direction tomorrow. An event or trend in nature, once identified, generally goes on forever, so linear, or inductive, logic makes the reasonable assumption that the future will resemble the past in a highly predictable fashion.

Linear logic is very useful for the natural sciences, but not for investing. The trends of the immediate past never extend into the indefinite future, although they may persist for many years. No asset—stocks, bonds, gold, real estate—goes up or down forever. Linear logic is not very useful in explaining why one investment trend ends or what trend will replace it, but another form of logic is.

Dialectic logic has a forbidding name, which is natural in light of its origin. A German philosopher named Hegel developed it, and another German philosopher named Marx vigorously exploited it. Both Hegel and Marx wrote in a ponderously Teutonic fashion which endears them only to masochistic readers who thrive on frustration. Behind its frustrating terminology, however, dialectic has two stellar virtues: it explains why trends change, and its basic ideas are reasonably simple.

Explaining why trends change is the major use of dialectic. Human events do not proceed in the neat, orderly fashion that events in the natural sciences do; instead they are filled with crises, turning points, and changes of direction. Dialectic recognizes this by starting with a trend (called a *thesis*) which goes forward under its own momentum until it reaches an extreme and then generates forces (called an *antithesis*) which deflect and change it. The clash of old trend and opposing forces creates a new trend (called a *synthesis*) which develops a life and momentum of its own and starts the process all over again. If this all seems a bit abstract, then consider a concrete example of one of the dominant trends of the last two generations: the trend toward greater government involvement in the economy, which began in the 1930s as the *solution* to the problem of the depression. After 50 years of growing power, government came to be viewed as the *cause* of problems such as inflation and excessive bureaucratic regulation.

The old trend toward greater government power generated conservative forces to oppose it. Margaret Thatcher and Ronald Reagan are the political results (and partially the political causes) of popular dissatisfaction with ever-expanding government power. The clash between the liberal momentum of growing government power and the rising tide of conservative opposition to it is producing a new attitude toward the proper role of government in the economy which will refocus and transform government power in the 1980s.

A major element of dialectic is recognizing that the solution to one problem (e.g., federal fiscal stimulus was the solution to the depression of the 1930s) generally goes to an extreme where it becomes the cause of another problem (e.g., too much fiscal stimulus became the cause of the inflation of the 1970s).

Merely recognizing that trends change confers a large advantage on an investor which is not shared by investors who take a linear view of the nonlinear investing world. Understanding why trends change confers a still larger advantage, which is the reason that a dialectic approach is employed in analyzing past investing games and why they ended. Dialectic is not difficult, but like any other new mode of thinking or acting, it takes a while to become accustomed to it. Lord Keynes expressed a similar idea in the introduction to his *General Theory of Employment, Interest, and Money:* "The difficulty lies, not in the new ideas, but in escaping from the old ones."[1]

# THE INFLUENCE OF KEYNES

For better and worse, the ideas of John Maynard Keynes have dominated twentieth-century economics. He went from heretic in the 1930s to savior in the 1960s and then on to villain in the 1970s, although his own life ended before he could see those last two stages. Because Keynes left such a large and enduring stamp on our time, many parts of the following chapters deal with the uses and abuses of his ideas.

# INVESTING AS A GAME

At first, investing seems too serious a subject to treat as a game. Money is at stake, often the money an investor needs to pay bills. On closer inspection, however, investing really does have many similarities to a game like tennis or golf.

Like any other game, investing has both winners and losers. The winners are those who learn the rules of the game they are playing and who diligently practice it until they are proficient. This book is a guide to the rules of the three major investing games open to investors.

---

[1]John M. Keynes, *The General Theory of Employment, Interest, and Money,* Harcourt Brace Jovanovich (Harbinger), New York, 1964, p. viii.

Like any other game, investing requires that players master themselves before they can win. Holding a golf club or tennis racket too firmly almost guarantees that an excited player will hit the ball some place other than where he wants it to go. The emotional investor who gets carried away with the euphoria of a bull market or the fear of a bear market is equally unlikely to make intelligent moves. Investing is a game which requires investors to become aware of their emotions and to master them.

Also like any other game, investing can be fun. It is an exciting intellectual challenge in a constantly changing world. Even the best investors miss often enough to keep them alert and interested in doing better the next time. There is enough room for improvement to last a lifetime. Unlike most other games, however, investing can be both fun and financially profitable to the good recreational player.

# CHAPTER TWO

# THE LAST NEGATIVE SUM ECONOMY

They said it could not happen. Conventional wisdom in 1929 said that permanent prosperity had been achieved and that economic collapse was impossible. In just 4 years 25 percent of the labor force was out of work in the worst economic catastrophe in the nation's history. Two generations later, Keynesian economists confidently believed that they too had banished the business cycle and guaranteed perpetual prosperity. Unfortunately no one can guarantee prosperity, and depressions are not only possible but necessary. A brief look at the causes of the last depression yields three conclusions about how another one might happen.

## CONFIDENCE ON THE EVE OF THE GREAT DEPRESSION

Like a Shakespearean tragedy, it began in triumph and ended in disaster.

There was much to feel triumphant about in 1929. The U.S. economy grew steadily through the 1920s and created a standard of living which was the envy of the world. The European economies never quite recovered from World War I, but that was the problem of the old world. The new world was showing the rest of the planet how it was done.

Confidence was the dominant mood of the country. It took confident entrepreneurs to borrow heavily to begin new enterprises and to expand existing ones. It took confident speculators to borrow heavily on the value of the stocks they bought while putting only a fraction of their own money down. It took confident bankers to make all those loans. But the country had confidence to spare.

The nation's confidence, like its wealth, was concentrated in a small segment of the population. Farmers spent most of the 1920s in their own private depression. Workers shared in the production of wealth during that decade, but not in its distribution and consumption. The newly created wealth largely flowed to business people and their shareholders.

Confidence was an essential precondition of the depression. Without it, business people and investors would not have taken the risks which left them so vulnerable when calamity struck. People generally prepare for the calamity they expect, but few in 1929 expected the hard times to come. They thought the party would last forever.

# THE PARTY ENDS

More than 50 years after the great depression of the 1930s began there is surprisingly little agreement among economists as to precisely what caused it. Most agree that the stock market crash of 1929 started the economic contraction and that well-intentioned blunders compounded it. The disagreement among economists revolves about the importance they attach to each of the blunders.

Stock market declines generally precede or accompany economic declines. In 1929 the stock market crash did more than herald the coming depression; it played a major role in causing it.

The stock market crash of 1929 quickly wiped out the equity of many leveraged investors. Shareholders who bought stocks on margin by putting up as little as 10 percent of their purchase price saw their equity disappear in a matter of days or even hours. Margin calls went out demanding that investors put up more cash or see their stocks sold. The forced sale of stocks to meet margin calls led to a cascade of sell orders, more margin calls, and more forced sales. It was a financial panic of the first order.

The financial panic was a microcosm of the human experience for observers who remained calm enough to avoid joining the rest of the crowd leaping out of Wall Street windows. Yesterday's heroes became today's fools and tomorrow's villains; Richard Whitney, president of the New York Stock Exchange, was jailed for fraud. Euphoria turned to despair and then to desperation. Previously rational persons did some very irrational things as their confidence crumbled. The stock market crash provided all the entertainment of a major military defeat, with one exception: only money was lost, not lives.

The spectacle of rich investors becoming poor rapidly was more than a melodrama. It set in motion a major contraction of aggregate demand in the economy. The stock market dropped 89 percent from its peak in 1929 to its low in 1932, quickly transforming the nouveau riche of the 1920s into the nouveau poor of the 1930s. Businesses which catered to the formerly wealthy suddenly found that the newly poor no longer could afford their goods and services. Workers who produced those goods and services found themselves unemployed. Business people who relied on the issue of new stock to finance their enterprises found both their finances and their businesses contracting.

Contracting demand cascaded through the economy just as selling pressure cascaded through the stock market. Businesses which no longer could sell their products also no longer could pay dividends to finance the consumption of their shareholders. Workers who became unemployed no longer could pay the corner grocer, who in turn no longer could pay the nation's already impoverished farmers. This cascading contraction of demand was a negative version of what Keynesian economists would later call the *multiplier effect.*

The stock market crash by itself probably would have caused a recession of average intensity. (*The Great Crash*, by J. K. Galbraith, provides an entertaining look at the impact of the stock market crash on the economy.)[1] Thanks to the mistakes of the leading politicians and best economists of the day, however, an average recession became a full-scale depression. With the best of intentions and most diligent of efforts, the prominent men in power produced the worst of results.

## THE BLUNDERS

The power of blunders to shape the course of human events is often vastly underestimated. No national leader intends that his actions bring disaster to his people with the rare exception of a misanthrope like Caligula who wished that all mankind had a single throat so that he might cut it. Most national leaders have good intentions, but unfortu-

---

[1]John K. Galbraith, *The Great Crash*, Houghton Mifflin, Boston, 1972.

nately good intentions are often nothing more than paving stones on the way to a well-known destination.

The Federal Reserve committed not one blunder but two. It allowed the nation's money supply to contract by one-third during the depression, an action which made an enormous contribution to the contraction of demand in the economy. Without money to spend, consumers and business people could not pay their debts and bills, let alone maintain their previous standard of living. Economists of the monetarist school of economics focus on this contraction of money as the prime cause of the depression.

The Fed's second mistake was to allow banks across the country to go under, dragging their depositors down with them. In 4 years, an incredible 44 percent of the nation's banks, mostly smaller ones, went to the wall. The banks' shareholders were expendable because they recognized (or should have) the normal and occasionally abnormal risks associated with share ownership. The depositors were not expendable, but many lost their savings and therefore their spending power. The depositors fortunate enough to keep their money often were too frightened to spend it as the terrifying depression deepened, a phenomenon Keynes called a *liquidity trap*. Devastated savers plus terrified spenders equaled a growing contraction of demand which pushed the economy even further in the abyss.

The Fed was not alone in its mistakes. Congress did its share by passing the Smoot-Hawley tariff in 1930. The intention was to save the jobs of U.S. workers. The actual result was to generate countervailing actions by other nations to build up tariff walls around their own markets. As each nation closed its door to other nations, world trade contracted, thereby adding to the great contraction of demand which dominated the 1930s. Seldom has there been such a stellar example of good intentions becoming awful results as the Smoot-Hawley tariff. Supply-side economists consider the tariff wars as a principal cause of the depression.

While Congress was precipitating the international trade war of the 1930s, Herbert Hoover was changing the English language. In a well-intentioned attempt to restore collapsing confidence, he avoided the emotionally charged words such as "crisis" and "disaster." Instead he substituted the then-innocuous term "depression" in an effort to calm the panic around him. The events of the 1930s became so bad, however, that the term "depression" came to mean the worst possible economic catastrophe.

Aside from changing the English language, Hoover did nothing of consequence. He correctly recognized the need to restore confidence, but did not know how to do it. He tried to balance the federal budget by cutting spending, but that just made one more contribution to the great contraction of demand. He took a passive approach to the crisis in the mistaken belief that a passive government would restore confidence to a laissez-faire economy capable of correcting its deficiencies. Unfortunately the economy was self-destructing rather than self-correcting, and Hoover's passive approach only engendered despair that no one was actively pursuing a solution to the depression. Hoover's good intentions were beyond doubt, and his relief work in Belgium after World War I proved him a compassionate humanitarian, but none of his good intentions saved him from the blunders which worsened the depression.

Judged by his campaign speeches, Franklin Roosevelt would have been no better able than Hoover in coping with the depression. He promised to cut federal spending by 25 percent, an action which would have made one more unnecessary contribution to the great contraction of demand. Once in office, Roosevelt promptly forgot his promises and started various spending programs. The penchant of politicians to say one thing and do another generally causes great cynicism among voters, but in this case Roosevelt was moving in the right direction to solve the great problem of his day. His movements toward fiscal stimulus were too small to do much good until World War II came along, but at least he was active in the right direction.

Roosevelt's activism was just what a shell-shocked nation needed. He tried one program after another, usually in the face of disapproval by the forces of conventional wisdom, including the Supreme Court, which ruled against some of his programs. Probably more important than his famous fireside chats (phrases such as "We have nothing to fear but fear itself" were perfect for the time) was the perception that someone in power was actually pursuing a solution to the great problem of depression.

The popular concept of passive, limited government died in the depression of the 1930s. From that point an active, growing government was perceived as the desirable solution to the nation's problems, particularly the problem of economic security. From under 10 percent in most cases in the early 1930s, government spending as a percentage of GNP rose to over 40 percent on both sides of the Atlantic by the 1980s. In Sweden and Holland where the welfare state bloomed in all its glory, government spending surpassed 60 percent of GNP before it generated enough popular force to stop its growth.

The new world had no monopoly on economic mistakes. The banking crisis of the depression was touched off by the failure of an Austrian bank. Germany went into depression early after hyperinflation made the mark worthless; the weak economy and the weaker democracy of the Weimar republic provided fertile ground for Hitler's brand of strong leadership. Britain returned to the gold standard at too high a level, forcing it to contract its own demand for imports to prevent an outflow of gold. Economic mistakes in other nations pushed down on world trade and made one more contribution to the great contraction of demand.

Economists still debate which of the above factors was the principal cause of the depression, a debate which is beyond the scope of this book. Debating the fine points of past policies is less important than extracting the principal lessons about what went wrong and how they might apply to the future. Those lessons are three:

**1.** *Contracting demand.* Aggregate demand for goods and services fell for a variety of reasons: impoverished shareholders no longer had money to spend; the money supply itself declined; the few people left with money were too frightened to spend it; etc. A future negative sum economy is likely to have different particular causes, but their impact will be determined by how much they depress the aggregate demand for goods and services.

**2.** *Crisis beyond control.* The economic crisis of the 1930s quickly moved beyond the ability of governments to control it, largely because they had very little power over the economy in comparison with governments today.

**3.** *Blunders made it worse.* The standard assumption today is that government actions will prevent a depression, but that assumption misses the fact that government actions in the 1930s were a major cause of depression. Good intentions and diligent actions led to awful results. Any future depression is likely to begin because of, and be made worse by, the blunders of the most respected persons in power. The fact that government has more power today than in the 1930s may mean that the mistaken use of that power will have an even greater negative impact in the future than it did in the past. A major reason that those in power made so many mistakes was that the nation's economists failed to give them adequate guidance. Most of the economists of the 1930s were not part of the solution to the great problem of their day; they were part of the problem itself.

# THE BREAKDOWN OF CONVENTIONAL ECONOMICS

Conventional economists of the 1930s had four problems: they did not recognize the problem of depression as it happened, did not think it was possible, did not understand its cause, and did not know how to solve it. Keynes's *General Theory*[2] remedied those deficiencies, but the book was not published until 1936 when the depression already was past its low point. Keynes's ideas were rejected as heresy by most of his peers; another generation went by before his ideas became the official orthodoxy.

At first many economists thought the problem was inflation, not depression. Industrial prices did move up in the boom of the late 1920s, leading many economists to think that curing inflation would be a major problem of the early 1930s. Their proposals to cut government spending, which would have been appropriate to fight inflation, just made the depression worse. Only when the economy went off a cliff did most economists identify the problem as depression.

The economists of the 1930s who reluctantly recognized the problem as depression generally did not recognize the cause of the problem as insufficient demand. Worse yet, they believed insufficient demand to be impossible. The reason for this willing denial of manifest reality was a law developed by a nineteenth-century Frenchman named Jean Baptiste Say. Discredited as it later came to be in the depression, Say's law was resurrected (rightly so in this author's opinion) by supply-side economists in the late 1970s to deal with an economy characterized by too much demand and not enough supply.

Say's law simply states that supply creates its own demand. When a farmer supplies 100 bushels of wheat to the market, he receives payment of $100. That payment allows the farmer to create demand of the same amount when he goes to the butcher, the baker, and the candlestick maker. If the farmer decides to save $20, he deposits it in a bank which lends it to someone else who spends it. Say proposed a simple, neat system where the supply of goods for $100 creates $100 in demand for other goods and services. Therefore, supply always equals demand.

What few economists of the 1930s recognized, however, is that there are some conditions under which $100 of supply will create less than $100 of demand. If the farmer who earns $100 for his wheat is simply scared stiff, as most people were during the 1930s, then he will spend only enough to satisfy his basic needs and will save the rest. He may spend only $75 and put the rest under a mattress. He is unlikely to deposit the remaining $25 in a bank, because banks are going bankrupt with distressing regularity. Even if he does deposit his funds with a bank, the bank is unlikely to lend the money to someone who will spend

---

[2]John M. Keynes, *General Theory of Employment, Interest, and Money,* Harcourt Brace Jovanovich (Harbinger), New York, 1964.

it, because the bankers are scared just as stiff and because creditworthy borrowers are few and far between. People simply were too frightened to spend their money, leading to a further contraction of demand. This hoarding behavior which reduced demand is Keynes's liquidity trap, mentioned earlier.

If the economists of the day did not recognize the problem of depression and did not understand its cause, then it is not surprising that they did not understand its solution. The world had changed, but the economists of the 1930s were unwilling or unable to change with it. As J. K. Galbraith later put it, "Economists are economical of ideas. They make the ones they learned in graduate school last a lifetime."[3] Given a choice between the ideas about Say's law they learned in graduate school and the reality of economic disintegration around them, most economists of the 1930s went to their graves still faithful to a dead Frenchman they never met. Noneconomists displayed a similar reluctance to change their thinking as the world changed around them, which led Keynes to comment, "Practical men who believe themselves to be quite exempt from any intellectual influences are generally the slaves of some defunct economist."[4]

In time Keynes himself would become a defunct economist who commanded the devotion of both practical men and professional economists who never quite understood that Keynes's ideas were right only for his time, not for all time. In his time, however, Keynes not only understood the great problem of depression; he saw a way out too.

## THE RISE OF KEYNES

Keynes is justly famous because he did three things right. He recognized the great problem of his day as depression. He recognized the cause of the problem as insufficient aggregate demand in the economy. And he recognized the solution as deficit spending to increase demand. All that sounds obvious now, but it was heresy to the conventional economists of the day and to Keynes himself.

A mark of a first-rate thinker is the ability to change his view of the world as the world changes around him. Keynes had the ability to discard the outdated ideas he had learned and to replace them with ideas more relevant to understanding the problems of his time. As he

---

[3]Lecture delivered at Harvard University, Cambridge, Mass., fall, 1972.

[4]John M. Keynes, op. cit., p. 283.

put it in the introduction to his *General Theory,* "I myself held with conviction for many years the theories which I now attack ... the composition of this book has been a struggle of escape—a struggle of escape from habitual modes of thought and expression."[5]

Keynes and his ideas were not accepted by the conventional economists of his day. He was dismissed as a speculator (Keynes used his knowledge of economics to make a great deal of money, a feat which economists then and now have trouble duplicating) rather than a serious thinker. Most of all, he was dismissed as a heretic to the sacred canons of economics.

Only a few young radicals embraced the heretical new ideas. The Keynesians, as they were later known, were caught up in the excitement and ferment of an idea whose time had come. Young Keynesians such as Paul Samuelson and J. K. Galbraith would become the most prominent economists of the next generation. Some of those young radicals who found the solution to the problem of depression and recession later became the old curmudgeons who helped cause the inflation of the 1970s.

Keynes's ideas on deficit spending were proved before they became accepted. World War II was financed by massive deficits which lifted the economy up and propelled it to a level of production barely believed possible at the time. The unemployed workers of the 1930s became the soldiers and sailors of the 1940s. A massive increase in military output took place with surprisingly little decrease in civilian output.

Like most new ideas, Keynesian economics did not triumph by convincing its opponents. It triumphed by outliving them. As the old economists retired or died, a new generation grew up which was far more comfortable with the new ideas. In the late 1960s Keynesian economics had completed the journey from heresy to orthodoxy. Most economists considered themselves Keynesians then, just as Keynes's ideas were becoming irrelevant. When President Nixon declared himself to be a Keynesian in 1971, the Keynesians already had made the transition from saviors of society to menaces of the economy, as later chapters will show.

Keynes would be only of historical interest except for the fact that his influence is still with us. Today Keynes is the defunct economist whose thoughts permeate the practical persons in power. His ideas were and are used to justify three of the major trends of the last 50 years which have become problems in their own right:

---

[5]Ibid., p. v.

1. The cancerous growth of government spending (including transfer payments) to over 40 percent of GNP in most western economies, up from a fraction of that figure 50 years ago.
2. The tendency of governments to live beyond their means by the use of perpetual deficits. Keynes's ideas made deficits seem not just acceptable but positively desirable. Even in the newly conservative governments of the 1980s, balanced budgets are usually projected and very seldom attained.
3. The rise of inflation as the great problem of the 1970s and possibly the 1980s as well. Growing governments financed themselves with growing deficits, and then printed money to cover those deficits.

## WHY WE MAY HAVE ANOTHER DEPRESSION

The reason a depression is necessary is disarmingly simple: neither history nor economic theory suggests any other way to stop the deeply embedded inflation which has become the great problem of our time. The economic contraction ending in late 1982 may be viewed as a "controlled depression" which sent unemployment into double digits to bring inflation down into single ones. The really interesting question is not whether economic pain is necessary to achieve price stability, but whether government can keep the pain under control or whether an uncontrolled financial crisis will erupt.

The causes and development of inflation are considered in the chapter on the zero sum economy. The conclusion is that inflation develops a powerful momentum of its own, much like a supertanker at sea. Newtonian mechanics describes how a good deal of time and energy are necessary to get a supertanker moving, and a comparable amount of time and energy must be applied in the opposite direction to stop it.

Inflation obeys an economic counterpart of Newtonian mechanics: the force necessary to stop it roughly corresponds to the force which set it in motion. Unfortunately, the western economies are all confronted by a deeply embedded inflation which is the product of many years and a great deal of energy. In the United States, the force which set inflation in motion was President Johnson's desire to have both a "great society" and a "great war" without raising taxes to pay for either one. The deficits and excessive credit creation to finance them continued through the 1970s, imparting a powerful momentum to inflation.

Turning around that deeply embedded inflationary momentum is a painful process. History is heavily on the side of one unpleasant conclusion: inflations do not have happy endings. From France after the revolution to Germany after World War I, inflationary booms have been followed by depressionary busts. Even the brief periods of moderate progress against inflation during the 1970s were the result of recession (often with a 1-year lag). There simply is no soft landing from a deeply embedded inflation.

Depression reduces inflation by changing both thought and the behavior which flows from that thought. As unemployment rises, labor thinks less about raises and more about job preservation. As the utilization of their industrial capacity falls, business people think less about raising prices and more about offering discounts to keep their customers. Inflation is more than a matter of too much money chasing too few goods; it is a way of thinking and acting as well. Only depression provides a force powerful enough to change the inflationary thoughts and actions of millions of workers, business people, and consumers.

Not that other ways to change inflationary thought and behavior have not been tried. Patriotism was the appeal of President Ford's WIN (whip inflation now) buttons, just as the worst recession in 40 years was beginning. Presidents Carter and Nixon both made anti-inflationary actions sound patriotic, but to little effect. Appeals to patriotism can be very effective against a foreign enemy, but not against a domestic one. The domestic identity of the inflationary culprit was revealed by Pogo: "We have met the enemy and he is us."

Wage and price controls (also called *incomes policy*) represented another futile attempt to lower inflation painlessly. The case for controls is that restricting the freedom of labor to raise wages and of business to raise prices will cure inflation without depression. Controls were popular in the mid 1970s but fell into disrepute for two good reasons: no one liked them and they simply did not work.

The tragedy of controls is that they might have worked when President Nixon first applied them in 1971. The shock of controls reduced inflationary expectations briefly and might have done so permanently if he had followed up with vigorous monetary and fiscal restraint. Instead he did the opposite to ensure his reelection the following year. Nixon had lost by a narrow margin to John Kennedy in 1960 partially because of the recession at the time, and he had no intention of repeating that mistake. Using controls to mask the buildup of inflationary pressures, he stimulated the economy and ensured two predictable outcomes: a resounding victory at the polls in 1972 and an explosion of inflation in 1973 to 1975.

The most reputable economists of our day have done their best to find a painless solution to inflation. They have failed. The Keynesians, at least what is left of them, spent most of the 1970s repeating their old catechism about how depressions are no longer possible; economists in the late 1920s suffered from the same delusion. Monetarists rightly focus on curtailing the growth of the money supply while downplaying the unpleasant side effects of that policy such as rising unemployment and bankruptcies. Despite the enormous intellectual energy spent in searching for alternative solutions or in ignoring the obvious one, the unpleasant fact remains that depression is the only proven cure for inflation. The worse the inflation, the worse the depression needed to cure it. The only real issue is whether the depression remains under government control or slips into financial crisis.

# THE RECENT CONTROLLED DEPRESSION

All past depressions have been involuntary and uncontrolled. The unique feature of the depression ending in late 1982 was that it remained under government control.

There is no generally accepted definition of depression. Recessions are determined officially by the National Bureau of Economic Research, but no organization draws the line between recession and depression. Professor Paul Samuelson once suggested that 10 percent unemployment in a developed economy[6] was a depression, and that definition will be used here if only for lack of any more accepted and precise one.

If we use 10 percent as the criterion, the U.S. economy slipped into depression in September of 1982, joining nations such as Britain, Belgium, and Holland, whose unemployment already was in double digits. U.S. capacity utilization was 70 percent and falling at the time, and was well under 50 percent in heavy industries such as autos and steels. Most other developed economies were in similar trouble.

History never repeats itself exactly, and the recent depression was far from an instant replay of the one in the 1930s. It was very tame, and for good reason. The recent depression was an attempt to use a controlled economic contraction to reduce inflation.

---

[6]Many lesser-developed countries have unemployment far higher than 10 percent.

So far the attempt has been successful. Inflation is down from the double digits of the late 1970s into mid single digits in most western economies. The cost is high in terms of unemployment, lost output, and bankruptcies, but the public outrage that once accompanied far lower rates of unemployment is notably absent. Most people, like most economists, seem to realize that the pain is a consequence of past excesses in economic policies just as a hangover is a normal consequence of excessive alcohol the night before.

The prime movers of this controlled depression are the developed world's central bankers. By keeping money tight and real interest rates at positive levels, they are trying to slow inflation over a period of years. The idea is that a medium amount of deflationary force applied over a long period of time will have the desired effect of lower inflation without letting the economy get out of control as it did in the 1930s. Given this menu of unpalatable options, controlled depression is probably the best choice if it works.

But no one knows whether it will work. About once every 4 years (the average business cycle is 49 months in length), central bankers have plunged their economies into recession to slow inflation, but they never have stayed the course long enough to drive inflation to zero. Whenever past recessions became too painful, they panicked and reflated their economies with a massive increase in the money supply which soon became a massive increase in inflation. This time, as in times past, central bankers say they will follow through until inflation is reduced to zero. The three possible outcomes of the current policy of controlled depression are:

1. It may succeed. Maybe central bankers will stay the course, and maybe the west's financial and economic system will hold together. If both those happy events take place, then the west's economies can become positive sum ones again in a few years. "My hope is that the depression should go on long enough that inflation has stopped completely" was how Nobel laureate Friedrich Hayek neatly summarized it.
2. It may lead to another round of reflation and double-digit inflation by the mid 1980s. Based on the past record of government's behavior during recessions, this is a likely outcome.
3. The controlled recession could become an uncontrolled one. Just as the political and economic leaders of the 1930s made well-intentioned blunders, the leaders of the 1980s may make mistakes which plunge our economy into the abyss. The first sign of an uncontrolled depression is likely to be a financial crisis which central bankers are powerless to stop.

# AN UNCONTROLLED DEPRESSION STARTS WITH A FINANCIAL CRISIS

Crises of all kinds wonderfully illuminate human nature. A financial crisis reveals the irrational ways people think and act when they face the loss of their money and their self-esteem which they often measure in monetary terms. Beyond its entertainment value and its insight into the behavior of people under pressure, a financial crisis is a major cause of uncontrolled depression.

Money is the glue binding millions of workers, consumers, and companies together in a modern economy. A financial crisis is the solvent which dissolves that glue. There is no lack of productive capacity in a depression—millions of workers want jobs and thousands of factories want orders—but the financial relationships which bind them all together become unstuck. By destroying wealth and the spending power which flows from that wealth, a financial crisis contracts aggregate demand and pushes the economy downward. The stock market crash began the destruction of wealth in the 1930s, and the collapse of many banks completed it. Consumers who were fortunate not to have their purchasing power wiped out were often too scared to use it. Business people who did not go bankrupt along with their customers often had neither the incentive nor the means to invest in new plant and equipment.

Each financial crisis takes a different form, but its impact on the economy generally comes through destroying financial assets and the confidence to spend them. If a financial crisis strikes in the 1980s, it is likely to take the form of insolvency rather than illiquidity. The distinction between a liquidity crisis and a solvency crisis becomes more apparent by analyzing the banking system.

A liquidity crisis is the classic bankers' nightmare. Most banks keep cash on hand equal to no more than 1 to 2 percent of deposits on the normally reasonable assumption that deposits and withdrawals will offset each other on a daily basis. When an abnormal number of frightened depositors rushes into the bank and demands their money right now, their demands may exceed the bank's money in the till. Without cash on hand to meet all its depositors' demands, the bank must shut its doors, a drastic step which usually causes panic and pandemonium among the remaining depositors. Given time, a solvent bank (i.e., one whose assets exceed its liabilities) can generate more cash by selling off its investments and allowing its loans to mature, but that is no comfort to the depositors left out in the cold.

Time can remedy a liquidity crisis, but not a solvency crisis. If a bank experiences losses equal to more than its capital and reserves, then it is insolvent and is no longer a viable business. It no longer can make new loans, and must run down its existing ones. Depositors are likely to pull their money out, particularly ones with deposits too large to be insured by the federal government. Since a money center bank generally has capital and reserves equal to 4 to 6 percent of assets, losses equal to more than that amount will render it insolvent and out of business.

When banks suffered both liquidity and solvency crises in the 1930s, the federal government resolved not to let it happen again. Federal deposit insurance now prevents frightened depositors from causing a run on the bank by assuring them that Uncle Sam stands behind their deposits. In the unlikely event that a bank does have liquidity problems, the Federal Reserve stands ready to lend it money through its rediscount window. Federal bank examiners enforce a host of regulations designed to keep banks out of trouble. The net result is to remove virtually any reasonable possibility that banks will suffer a liquidity crisis today.

No such federal assurance applies to a potential solvency crisis. If a large number of banks are imprudent enough to lose their capital, then there is not much the Federal Reserve or any other agency can do about it. The next section describes how a solvency crisis might start and how it might bring about an uncontrolled depression.

# A POSSIBLE SOLVENCY CRISIS

Lightning and loan losses seldom strike the same place twice. Loan losses struck conglomerates in the 1970 recession and hit oil tankers and real estate investment trusts in 1973 to 1975. Today the most likely candidates for loan losses are lesser-developed countries (LDCs) which means that the power to create an international financial crisis now lies with nations which are poor and weak. The most likely scenario is that LDCs will honor loans to U.S. bankers, but that scenario requires the active cooperation of people who really don't like them very much.

U.S. bankers normally assume that the federal government will relieve them of the logical consequences of their own imprudence. When loan losses begin to mount in a recession, bankers anxiously expect monetary and fiscal stimulus to cure it. A rising economic tide refloats all but the most leaky of beached corporate boats, but occasionally there are some companies in so much trouble that even a brisk recovery from recession is insufficient to save them. In extreme cases such as Lockheed and Chrysler, the federal government steps in with loan guarantees which bail out the banks in addition to saving the company. While the specific loan problems vary from one recession to the next, the general pattern of federal assistance to banks in trouble remains the same: reflation of the economy and guarantees of loans.

Bankers adopt a posture of coercive vulnerability in successfully securing federal aid. After making so many imprudent loans that their survival is at stake, bankers plead for federal assistance. They claim that terrible things will happen to the country if the banks (and, of course, the bankers) are allowed to go under. Grudgingly that assistance usually comes forth, particularly from the Federal Reserve. Like a driver who swerves to avoid a blind or drunk pedestrian, the Fed generally swerves from its tight money policy when it sees vulnerable bankers stumbling across the road.

Because federal power rescued bankers from past problem loans, the bankers naturally assume that it will rescue them from future problem loans as well. Currently the most likely future problems in bank loans are in LDCs, which are collectively in debt to the extent of about $500 billion.[7] (Mexico and Brazil are the largest debtors, with about $80 billion each.) While some of these debts represent direct government credit or loans from the World Bank, 53 percent is commercial bank lending. That amounts to a quarter-trillion dollars at risk, which far exceeds the capital and reserves of most large U.S. banks. In Mexico alone, banks such as Manufacturers Hanover and Bank of America have over 70 percent of their capital at risk.

If LDCs are to make good on their enormous loans, they must have both the ability and willingness to repay them. Today their ability to repay their loans is in doubt, and tomorrow their willingness may be in doubt too. Unlike the case with domestic loans, federal power has major limits when it comes to rescuing bankers from their own imprudence.

Most LDCs simply have no practical ability to repay their loans with exports. Their markets in developed countries are depressed by deepening recession and rising protectionism. Debt service takes over 50 percent of export earnings of countries from Argentina to Yugoslavia, and much of that debt is short-term. (Brazil is a notable exception. Most of its debt is medium-term and is not coming due soon. Ireland, while not an LDC, also has extended maturities on a debt that amounts to 60 percent of its GNP.) Most LDCs already are in depressions themselves, with unemployment far into double digits; they are unable to meet the

---

[7] *Wall Street Journal,* 8 Nov. 1982.

basic economic needs of their own people let alone the demands of their foreign bankers.

Strange as it may seem at first, the inability of LDCs to repay their debts is not very disturbing to U.S. bankers. Most bankers never really expected to be repaid, particularly on short-term loans. They expected their loans would be "evergreen" just as U.S. Treasury debt is: always rolled over but never paid off. Rolling over short-term debts also produces syndication fees for the banks and more work to justify the salaries of highly paid international bankers.

The problems with the evergreen approach to LDC loans are more apparent now than when the loans were made. A foreign government cannot tax its citizens in dollars to repay its dollar debts the way our own U.S. Treasury taxes us. A foreign government cannot print more dollars to pay its debts the way our own government can and does. Last, a foreign government may be unable to roll over its debts if banks lose confidence, a situation which currently exists in Poland.

## PAST FOREIGN DEFAULTS

The evergreen approach to foreign lending seemed harmless in light of another cherished banker's belief—that nations are eternal and therefore cannot disappear into bankruptcy the way a corporate borrower can. If history had begun with the end of World War II, that optimistic view of sovereign risks would be justified. Except for Cuba in 1962, the postwar record is remarkably free of governments repudiating their debts. Countries in trouble generally roll over their debts, often with help from the International Monetary Fund, and the game goes on as before. A longer view of history, however, reveals a very different view of sovereign risk loans.

There were two waves of foreign loan defaults in the nineteenth century and another in the 1930s. From the depths of the depression in 1933 came an excellent summary of what periodically happens to sovereign risk loans:

> Adjustments will be made. Debt will be scaled down and nations
> will start anew. The investor will receive sufficiently satisfactory
> explanations as to how it is to his advantage to accept new
> promises in place of ones which were repeatedly broken. All will at
> last be forgotten. New foreign loans will once again be offered, and
> bought as eagerly as ever. They will give more unreliable
> information, and the process known for more than two thousand
> years will be continued. Defaults will not be eliminated. Investors

will once again be found gazing sadly and drearily upon foreign promises to pay.[8]

Ultimately the failure of foreign governments to repay their loans depends only partially on their inability to do so. As long as bankers are willing to go on rolling over existing loans including accrued interest, no loss need be recognized. A willing suspension of disbelief is necessary when bankers pretend that nothing is wrong with borrowers who can't repay their loans, but that is just the way the game is played. The risk that the game will end comes when at least one of two events occurs: bankers become too frightened to go on rolling over their loans or the borrower simply refuses to pay.

The first of those two events to end the foreign lending game took place in Poland, a subject covered later in this chapter. In November 1981, just as bankers became too frightened to lend more to Poland, Alfredo Phillips, deputy director of Banco de Mexico summarized the rosy situation of his own nation as the darling of the world's bankers: "We are still being sought out by bankers. Countries with access to the market, like Mexico, can borrow any amount of money. If your credit standing is good—like ours—you can continue to increase your debt."[9] Only months after he spoke those words, Mexico was in de facto default.

The causes of Mexico's trouble were classic. Mexico overborrowed on the assumption that its income (in this case from oil) would go up forever. When trouble came, it came in battalions (e.g., oil volume and oil prices both declined, and the world recession hit other exports). Eventually confidence in Mexico began to crumble, starting with the confidence of its own people who moved their pesos into dollars. The trickle of fleeing pesos became a torrent and turned into a run on the Mexican central bank. With its current account deficit expanding and its currency reserves shrinking, Mexico nationalized its own banks and desperately tried to stem the hemorrhage of dollars.

There is no way to predict in advance precisely when economic mismanagement will cause bankers' confidence to collapse. In Mexico's case, confidence disappeared in the summer of 1982. Bankers no longer wanted to roll over their largely short-term loans, but they had little choice since Mexico had no way to repay them. Bankers were upset at

[8]Max Winkler, *Foreign Bonds—An Autopsy,* Roland, Swain, Philadelphia, 1933, p. 179.

[9]Alfredo Phillips, *Institutional Investor,* November 1981, p. 305.

the Mexicans for not repaying their loans, and the Mexicans were just as upset at them. One Mexican banker said of the bankers who lent his country money, "Those bastards got us into this hole. Now they are trying to bleed us for everything we have."[10]

## WHY NATIONS DEFAULT

The idea that distressed debtors actually might hate their bankers is not as surprising as it seems at first. Prudence in banking requires that a banker keep loans to a reasonable level which causes no great pain to the borrower, but by that standard U.S. bankers clearly have been imprudent in their loans to LDCs. Repaying loans causes LDCs a great deal of deflationary pain, and they deeply resent the lenders who force that pain on them. The relationship of banker and distressed borrower is like that of drug dealer and drug addict: dependency mixed with resentment and disrespect.

If LDCs hate anyone more than their bankers, the likely candidate is the International Monetary Fund (IMF). The IMF is widely (and correctly) regarded as the agent of rich nations in dealing with poor nations in financial trouble.[11] The IMF offers loans with deflationary conditions attached, which generally translates into lower GNP and higher unemployment for the nations which accept those conditions. Many of the IMF's conditions are necessary, but virtually all of them are painful. The spectacle of rich nations forcing painful austerity measures on poor nations is not one of the more ennobling sights in international finance, but it does help bankers get their money back. It comes as no surprise that bankers are usually vigorous supporters of the IMF when it forces LDCs to do unpleasant things to their own people.

To their credit (as a banker would use that term), LDCs are behaving honorably toward their debts. Faced with a choice of inflicting the pain of deflation on their voters or the pain of default on their U.S. bankers, LDCs are choosing the former. Brazil's recession of 1981 to 1982 was largely an attempt to please its U.S. bankers. By late 1982 Brazil's economic planners went to the extreme of using their estimate of foreign borrowings as the major factor in managing their economy; other factors such as growth and unemployment were relegated to secondary status.

---

[10] *Wall Street Journal,* 22 Oct. 1982.

[11] To be fair, not all of the IMF's loans are to poor countries, but poor countries are where most of the problem loans are located.

Like misery, bankruptcy loves company. Fortunately for U.S. bankers, there is not yet any serious talk of a debtors' cartel to orchestrate a mass default on their loans. Like penguins jostling each other on an Antarctic ice shelf, no major nation wants to be the first to plunge into default. If one major borrower does take the plunge, however, others will be much less reluctant to follow it. Bankers have a large incentive to prevent the first major default, which could be the tip of an iceberg which tears a hole in their vulnerable side.

Preventing a major sovereign risk default requires LDCs to believe that the evil of default on their debts is worse than the evil of deflating their economies. Like lawyers, bankers argue their side of the case by threatening to cut off trade credits and future access to the world's financial markets. Like judges, the LDCs have the power to agree with their U.S. bankers or to refuse to pay them.

As judges, the LDCs can choose to default for both economic and political reasons. The obvious economic reason is the desire to dispense with the pain of deflating their economies and diverting their scarce resources to pay their foreign bankers. There is no scientific way to predict when a debt burden becomes intolerable, but Keynes summarized the classic debtor's decision: "The active and working elements in no community, ancient or modern, will consent to hand over to the rentier or bondholding class more than a certain proportion of the fruits of their work."[12]

Political reasons add to economic ones as an LDC ponders whether to default. When revolution swept Iran after the fall of the shah, members of the Revolutionary Council threatened to default on their debts to the "Great Satan," as Iranian religious leaders called the United States. Fortunately for U.S. bankers, Iranian bank deposits neatly offset Iranian loans, so the threatened default merely became a complicated and still continuing process of using Iranian assets to cancel Iranian obligations. Unfortunately for U.S. bankers, however, virtually all other LDCs have debts far exceeding their deposits, so another such happy ending is very unlikely.

The enormous outpouring of Iranian hostility toward the United States came as a surprise to many people, but the potential for similar hostility exists elsewhere too. Black Africans resent our tilt toward South Africa. Turks resent our tilt toward Greece over Cyprus. Latin Americans have long memories for real and imagined wrongs inflicted on them by the Colossus of the North. For Argentines who feel bitter

---

[12]John M. Keynes, *The Collected Writings of John Maynard Keynes*, vol. 4: *A Tract on Monetary Reform*, Macmillan, New York, 1971, chap. 2.

over our tilt toward Britain in the Falklands war of 1982, only a short memory is necessary.

Many LDCs have particular reasons to dislike the United States, but most feel the age-old resentment the poor generally have for the rich. Napoleon observed that religion is what keeps the poor from murdering the rich, and today there is a growing number of apostates to the commercial religion which U.S. bankers take for granted. When the United States had half the world's GNP and a near monopoly of its nuclear weapons, a situation which prevailed at the middle of this century, U.S. bankers could safely assume that U.S. power would force other nations to respect their assets held abroad and to pay back their loans.

## THE EFFECTS OF DEFAULT

The situation is very different today. Bankers no longer can expect the Marines to go into nations in default as they did in banana republics at the turn of the century. As U.S. power began to wane in the closing days of Vietnam, oil-producing nations seized assets of U.S. oil companies, a step which would have been unthinkable when U.S. power was at its zenith. Just as the protective umbrella of U.S. power began to fold in the 1970s, U.S. bankers made the anomalous decision to increase their assets at risk abroad. That decision now gives the power to prevent or precipitate a world financial crisis to leaders who run countries which are poor, weak, and more than a little desperate.

Confronted by LDCs in default, there is little bankers can do but complain that the LDCs are not playing by the made-in-USA rules of international finance which bankers have come to take for granted. Normally a bank recovers most of a bad debt by seizing and selling the borrower's collateral (large banks have special departments dedicated to working out problem loans), but that avenue may be closed in the case of an LDC. There is little collateral for the banks to seize, so there is a significant chance that problem loans to LDCs in default will be total losses.

A major loss on loans to LDCs (or any other problem loan) would find banks far less prepared than a generation ago. The old bankers who survived the depression of the 1930s (many did not) built their banks into financial fortresses with high-quality assets and strong capital positions. The younger bankers who replaced them aggressively reduced the quality of their banks' assets by replacing risk-free Treasury obligations with risk-laden loans, including loans to LDCs. Those aggressive bankers also increased the leverage on their bankers' capital; $1 of bank capital supports $11 in loans today, versus supporting only $4 in loans 30 years ago. Reduced asset quality and rising capital leverage combine to lower the cushion which separates a bank from insolvency.

An insolvent bank cannot continue to operate. It cannot extend new loans to finance another round of credit-based economic recovery and inflation. It must contract its existing loans to correspond to its contracted equity base. In short, an insolvent bank is out of business. Companies, consumers, and countries which have relied on the bank to finance their growth and current living standards suddenly find that their growth is going into reverse and that their living standards are shrinking. If the insolvent bank's customers must reduce their loans, then aggregate demand in the economy is being reduced as well. If only one bank were affected by loan losses, then other banks could take up the slack, but a wave of LDC defaults would put many money center banks in solvency trouble.

When banks get in trouble, they run to the Federal Reserve for help. Because the Fed failed to help in the 1930s and even made the situation worse, Fed officials today are anxious to avoid criticism for starting another depression. Despite their good intentions (Fed officials in the 1930s had good intentions too), there are several possible pitfalls:

Central bankers are as anxious to avoid criticism for another round of inflation as to avoid criticism for another depression. Their goal of avoiding inflation may lead them to overstay their restrictive monetary policies until it is too late to control the situation.

Central bankers are better at responding to a liquidity crisis than to a solvency crisis. They are well prepared to fight the last war of illiquidity, but they do not have any obvious weapons to fight a war in which major banks are becoming insolvent because of large loan losses.

Confusion may bring down the international financial system, since no one is clearly in charge of it. If a Japanese bank operating in the Bahamas takes U.S. dollar deposits from Kuwaiti depositors and lends them to Polish borrowers who then default, which central bank is in charge of the rescue operation? The huge pool of money which makes up the Eurodollar market (about $1 trillion, but a large and uncertain part of that sum represents interbank deposits rather than loans to ultimate customers) blurs the lines of responsibility as to who is in charge. In a crisis, no one may be in charge. A recent example of this sort of confusion came when Italy's central bank chose not to stand behind the obligations of Banco d' Ambrosias foreign branches.

Beyond central banks such as our own Federal Reserve, there are two other organizations which provide a degree of relief: the World Bank and the International Monetary Fund. The World Bank generally makes long-term development loans to LDCs, a worthy mission in theory although occasionally a controversial one in practice. From a commercial banker's standpoint, the World Bank is helpful in providing more credit to distressed LDCs. By tying their default clauses to World Bank loans, commercial bankers try to make LDCs more reluctant to default.

While the IMF lends money to LDCs too, its prime role is not development but crisis management. For a nation in financial trouble, the IMF provides temporary loans with strong conditions attached. As mentioned earlier, the IMF's deflationary conditions are very unpopular among LDCs which are improverished already.

The power of the World Bank and IMF to prevent a financial crisis is important but far from invincible. Recently the IMF increased its contributions by 50 percent from rich countries, including a reluctant United States. For many LDCs this additional source of borrowing power simply means an even more crushing burden of debts added to the ones they are unable to pay now. The *real* burden of LDC debts is still growing because the real rate of interest they pay is still sharply positive, which is a dramatic contrast to past business cycle recoveries when the Fed's easy money policy inflated away the real value of debts by driving real interest rates to negative levels. While IMF loans put distressed LDCs even further in the hole in real terms, there is no scientific way to predict when those LDCs will conclude that they can't take the pain any more, will default, and will cause a major financial crisis.

The domestic impact of a financial crisis depends on how dependent the rest of the economy is on debt to finance its activities. If corporate balance sheets were as strong today as they were just after World War II, then a financial crisis in the banking system would have only limited impact on the rest of the economy. Unfortunately the same aggressive and optimistic psychology which impelled bankers to increase leverage on their own balance sheets also impelled corporate managers to do the same (see the table on pretax interest coverage, page 148). Today most corporations are addicted to debt and therefore would be very vulnerable if the flow of new debt were to be cut off in a financial crisis.

"A claim on the smile of the Cheshire cat" is how Fed board member Henry Wallich summarized U.S. bank claims on LDCs. The most likely scenario is that the LDC loans will be rolled over and that U.S. banks will emerge a bit nervous but otherwise no worse for wear. The most likely scenario is not, however, the only possible one. In the event that one or more LDCs flatly repudiate their debts, then several large U.S. banks will become insolvent and the international financial system as we know it may slowly (or rapidly) disappear. In a world economy where consumers, companies, and countries are so addicted to debt, any sharp halt in the steady flow of that debt can cause severe withdrawal pains in the form of a worldwide *uncontrolled* depression.

# EUROPE'S POTENTIAL
# FINANCIAL CRISIS

"Those loans are unquestioned" was the way a West German banker described his views of borrowings by the Soviet Union and its satellites to me in 1979. Few people would describe them in such glowing terms today, and there is little excuse for ever having done so. Worthless czarist war bonds are this century's best example of how a nation can default for political reasons as well as economic ones.

For over a decade eastern Europeans exploited hopes about detente and peace by infusing their own flagging economies with western Europe's technology and capital goods. Even better from their standpoint, they paid for much of their imports from the west with credits extended by western governments and banks. Since most of the credits came from western Europe, U.S. banks are blissfully underexposed to defaults from the centrally planned economies of eastern Europe.

As with LDCs, eastern European countries can default for economic reasons or political ones. Poland is in de facto default for economic reasons despite the earnest attempts of its government to pay its debts. Poland borrowed over $25 billion from the west to buy large amounts of capital and technology which simply did not work well, particularly in the disruptions which followed the rise of the Solidarity union.

Other eastern European countries are having similar but smaller problems in servicing their debts, even East Germany which has been the communist bloc's powerhouse. Many of the economic difficulties are unique to the communist bloc, but two are shared with LDCs: interest rates are now high in real terms, and the recession in developed western countries limits the ability of debtors to pay their debts with exports.

Perhaps more important than the economic risk is the political one. Detente is not likely to last forever with a territorially ambitious and ideologically hostile nation such as the Soviet Union. Despite their history of almost constant warfare, most Europeans cannot conceive of a situation where their treasured detente crumbles into a new cold war or even into a hot one. The current generation of Soviet leaders seems cautious enough not to heat up the conflict between east and west, but the death of Brezhnev vividly demonstrates that the old generation will not last forever. A new and more active generation may recognize that they have the power to cause financial chaos in the west by defaulting on their debts to western banks and that using that power is to their advantage.

The classic banker J. P. Morgan once remarked that a borrower's character is more important than his cash flow or collateral. It is one thing to lend money to countries such as Britain and Germany which share our sense of commercial morality, including a borrower's obligation to repay debts. It is a very different thing to lend money to an LDC which may have no well-developed sense of commercial morality or to a nation such as the Soviet Union whose morality actively hopes for the destruction of the capitalist system which made the loan possible. Even if LDCs and eastern Europe were in sound economic condition, which they are not, their doubtful character should have suggested far more caution and prudence than bankers employed in making loans to them.

## TIMING, MISTAKES, AND SURPRISE

Predicting when and where a financial crisis will strike is like predicting when and where a rubber band will break. An observer can see that it is being stretched tighter and tighter, but cannot predict where or when it will snap. Predicting an uncontrolled depression with pinpoint accuracy is even more difficult because it is a once in a lifetime event —which is of little comfort today, since the last uncontrolled depression was almost a lifetime ago.

Perhaps the major danger in timing an uncontrolled depression is to expect it too soon, lose confidence with oneself and credibility with others, and throw in the towel just before it strikes. The world's economic and financial system has proved to be very resilient so far, and it may be that way for some time to come. When an uncontrolled depression does strike, it may come swiftly and by surprise.

The collapse of the stock market in 1929 came as a surprise, and the event which precipitates the next uncontrolled depression may come as a surprise too. Despite the wide recognition of the dangers inherent in LDC loans, an outright repudiation of debt by Mexico or Brazil would come as a real shock to bankers and investors. Perhaps the financial crisis which sets off an uncontrolled depression will come later in the decade from an entirely different quarter, but almost certainly it will spread quickly to destroy confidence. The speed with which confidence can collapse was demonstrated by Mexico, which took less than a year to go from banker's darling to basket case.

If a surprise event which triggers a depression cannot be predicted, then neither can the mistakes which make it worse. The uncontrolled depression of the 1930s was due at least as much to the blunders of those in power as to the economic and financial problems they faced. Those who committed those blunders held high positions, had excellent credentials, and possessed only the vaguest understanding of the crisis in which they were victims, participants, and causes. Frightened leaders under pressure are almost certain to make mistakes, but not always the same mistakes. The protectionist trend among developed countries is a mild (so far) version of the deflationary Smoot-Hawley tariff, but present parallels to past events are as likely to be misleading as helpful. The universe of potential mistakes is a huge one, and some new and unique mistakes are likely to exacerbate any future uncontrolled depression.

## SIGNS OF ANOTHER UNCONTROLLED DEPRESSION

No bell rang to announce the last uncontrolled depression, and no bell will ring to announce the next one. There are, however, four indicators which an investor can use to determine the economy's vulnerability to another uncontrolled depression.

1. *The monetary indicator.* A high real rate of interest is the best measure of tight money. A simple way of measuring real interest rates is to compare the current prime rate charged by banks (and listed daily in the *Wall Street Journal*) with the latest 12 months' increase in the consumer price index (CPI). When the prime rate exceeds the CPI by more than 5 percent, an investor may conclude that money is tight enough to trigger deflationary forces.

Deflationary forces were unleashed in October 1979 when the Federal Reserve switched its operating policy from controlling interest rates to controlling the growth of the money supply. Real interest rates went to the 10 percent area, which prompted West Germany's chancellor Helmut Schmidt to exclaim that they were the "highest since Jesus Christ walked the earth." High real interest rates were transmitted around the globe through the world's capital markets and made a powerful contribution to the double-digit unemployment rates which many western countries suffered in 1982. How long real interest rates will remain positive is the major issue in monetary policy.

If the practical definition of money were stable, then tracking the current growth of the money supply would produce an excellent leading indicator of future inflation. Because the definition of money is changing owing to money market accounts and the deregulation of interest rates, however, just what constitutes the money supply is open to question. The safest approach is to use M3, which is a broad enough measure of the money supply to avoid the changes currently affecting M1 and M2. If M3 grows faster than the 2 to 3 percent long-term growth potential of the economy, then more infation is likely. If M3 grows at a double-digit rate on a year-over-year basis (short-term swings can be misleading), then significant inflation is the likely outcome.

2. *The fiscal indicator.* If the federal government's budget deficit exceeds 2 percent of GNP, then an investor may conclude that fiscal policy is stimulating aggregate demand in the economy rather than reducing it. If a balanced budget is passed *and* implemented (unlikely in the author's opinion), then the budget deficit will disappear into a hail of tax increases and spending cuts. With fiscal policy essentially neutral, one of the main stimulants to both inflation and economic activity would be gone.

3. The *financial indicator.* The presence of a major financial excess whose collapse could touch off deflationary pressures is a sign that the economy is vulnerable to depression. The collapse of the speculative bubble in stocks touched off the uncontrolled depression of the 1930s, and the collapse of speculative lending to LDCs could touch off an uncontrolled depression in the 1980s. There is no certainty that any particular speculative bubble will burst (e.g., the speculative bubble in real estate during the late 1970s collapsed slowly but painfully in the early 1980s), but the potential for financial panic is far greater when a major financial excess is present. Currently the LDC loans of money center banks are the most visible financial excess.

4. *The political indicator.* This is the least precise indicator, but by no means the least important. The political willingness to tolerate either rising unemployment or rising prices determines whether fiscal and monetary policies will be tight or loose. A glacial shift toward price stability signals the rising political will to prevent inflation from becoming awful, but so far there does not seem to be enough political will to end inflation completely.

# A DEPRESSION IS NOT ALL BAD

Lost output, lost jobs, and lowered living standards are the costs of depression. But a depression has its benefits too. It forces companies to control their costs more carefully and to cut out the fat which frequently accumulates during an economic boom; when business at last picks up at companies which have tightened their belts, that business is likely to be run more productively and profitably. Economists such as Joseph Schumpeter and Jay Forrester have pointed out that the technologies which enable an economy to boom during an expansion often were developed during the preceding depression.

No depression, controlled or uncontrolled, lasts forever, even though prosperity may be a long way around the next corner. While it lasts, a depression reduces current inflation and expectations of future inflation. It restores corporate balance sheets to health either through bankruptcy (which wipes out past debts) or through motivating frightened corporate treasurers to be far more conservative in managing their liabilities. In short, a depression lays the financial groundwork for a future positive sum economy. While the depression is under way, however, it creates a great opportunity to play the negative sum investing game.

# CHAPTER THREE

# THE NEGATIVE SUM INVESTING GAME

Inflation will not last forever, strange as that may seem at first to the generation under 35 which has no adult experience with anything but a continuously rising consumer price index. Unfortunately the only sure cure for a deeply embedded inflation is a deeply painful depression. Using 10 percent unemployment as a relevant definition of depression, many western economies (including our own) were there already as 1983 began. A depression, controlled or uncontrolled, creates a negative sum investing game. The winners and losers in a negative sum investing game are the subject of this chapter.

The destruction of real wealth is the dominant trend of a negative sum investing game.[1] From an investor's standpoint, that destruction takes place in three dimensions:

The economy declines in real terms, so there are fewer goods and services to go around. The entire nation is worse off, but some parts much more so than others. As in a game of musical chairs, the object is not to be left standing when the music of inflation finally stops playing.

---

[1]By contrast, the transfer of real wealth is the dominant trend of a zero sum investing game, and the creation of real wealth is the dominant trend of a positive sum investing game.

Asset prices decline. The high real interest rates which accompany a recession lower the present value of all assets that assume a future stream of income (e.g., stocks, bonds, and real estate). High real interest rates break the value of non-income-producing assets (e.g., gold, stamps, and art) by reducing the probability of future price appreciation and raising the costs of carrying them with debt.

High real interest rates reduce the *certainty* of receiving future income and of its present value. Bankruptcies rise in depressions, raising the risk that shareholders will not get their dividends and bondholders will not get their interest. Investors threatened with bankruptcy frequently sell their assets such as stocks to pay their debts, raising the risk of a bear market. The sight of borrowers going bankrupt frightens lenders into demanding higher rates of interest as the price of bearing higher risk; in extreme cases it becomes a vicious circle where creditors are willing to lend money only at interest rates that borrowers are unable to afford.

## CONVENTIONAL WISDOM

Conventional wisdom, as usual, is likely to be misleading. The most respected preachers of conventional wisdom generally attain their prestigious positions during the previous positive or zero sum investing game and are unlikely to see their favorite game coming to an end. Yale's Irving Fisher made notable contributions to monetary theory, but not to the profits of investors who followed his advice just before the great stock market crash in 1929:

> Stock prices have reached what looks like a permanently high plateau.... I expect to see the stock market a good deal higher than it is today, within a few months.[2]

Bernard Baruch was one of the most celebrated speculators on Wall Street, but his hopeful comment printed in *American Magazine* was not very helpful to investors:

---

[2]J. K. Galbraith, *The Great Crash*, Houghton Mifflin, Boston, 1972, p. 75.

The economic condition of the world seems on the verge of a great forward movement.[3]

Baruch himself managed to emerge from the depression with his reputation and finances reasonably intact, but not many other speculators were as fortunate.

Baruch was also the author of the adage that bears don't own houses on Fifth Avenue. He might have added that being a bear simply is not much fun even when it is profitable. The successful investment adviser during a negative sum investing game is regarded as a prophet of doom, which is a label few people have the temperament to wear for very long, if at all.

## THE LOSERS—DEBTORS

"Neither a borrower nor a lender be" was Shakespeare's classic but wrong advice. Being a borrower makes a great deal of sense during an inflationary economy when an investor can deduct the interest on his or her tax return, repay the debt in cheaper dollars, and enjoy capital gains on the investments made with borrowed money. Those advantages of being a borrower decline or even disappear when interest rates go up and inflation comes down.

Debts cannot be repaid in cheaper dollars without inflation to make them cheaper. The general price level in the economy actually declined during the 1930s, so debtors had to repay their borrowings in *more* expensive dollars. A modern version of the same problem is when the interest rate on the debt exceeds the general level of inflation by a significant margin; that requires the borrower to repay in *relatively more* expensive dollars. In real terms the borrower loses.

Even more important than the general level of inflation in the economy is the particular rate at which an investor's assets and income are going up. Borrowing at 10 percent in an economy with inflation of 5 percent still makes sense if investors are fortunate enough to have investments with a reasonable prospect of a 20 percent return or if they expect their income to go up at 20 percent per year. If their investments go down instead of up or if they lose their jobs and income, then

[3]Ibid.

they are in trouble. *Investors guarantee the payment of principal and interest on their debts, but seldom does anyone reliable guarantee the investors that they will receive the appreciation in assets or income that they hoped to obtain.* Not all debts are created equal. Borrowers with short-term debts will find their interest rates going down along with inflation. Corporations with high-coupon bonds and investors with high-interest mortgages will find themselves paying a large real rate of interest longer than they would like. Given enough time and prepayment penalties, a bond or mortgage can be refinanced at a lower interest rate, but that is seldom an instant or painless process.[4]

The tax advantages of debt are still present in a negative sum investing game, but are much less relevant. The relevant question is often, Deductible from what? If the investor's assets or income decline in a depression, there is much less from which to deduct interest. The real aftertax rate of interest also goes from negative to positive as inflation declines. In both cases in the accompanying table, the real rate of interest is 3 percent and the tax rate is 50 percent.

| | Inflationary economy, % | Noninflationary economy, % |
|---|---|---|
| Inflation rate | 7.0 | 0 |
| Nominal rate of interest | 10.0 (7 + 3) | 3.0 (0 + 3) |
| Aftertax rate of interest | 5.0 | 1.5 |
| Real aftertax rate of interest | −2.0 (5 − 7) | 1.5 (1.5 − 0) |

The worst possible case for an investor is to borrow long term at a high rate of interest to buy an asset with low or negative current income (many real estate investors in the late 1970s bought properties with negative cash flows), which cannot cover the interest payments. If depression prevents income on the asset from rising (or worse yet, causes it to decline), then the investor loses money as long as he or she holds the asset. If depression causes the price of the asset to decline (most asset prices will go down in a depression), then the investor loses when selling it too.

---

[4]Veterans Administration mortgages are a pleasant exception. High-coupon mortgages can be refinanced with low-coupon ones quickly and at low cost to the borrower.

Consumers who have no investments may find themselves in trouble too. The prevailing American consumer ethic of "buy now before it goes up" makes little sense when prices are no longer going up. Since interest rates on consumer debt tend to be high under the best of circumstances, paying them tends to keep debt-laden consumers deeply in debt, which is just where their creditors normally want them. If the consumers lose their jobs in a depression, however, then both they and their creditors are in trouble.

Debt acts as a neutral magnifying glass. When things go well, debt magnifies the gain. When things go badly, debt magnifies the loss. Since most things will be going badly in a depression, minimizing debt is a good general investment policy.

## THE LOSERS—REAL ESTATE

There is a myth that real estate never declines in value, a myth believed by investors with short and selective memories. Real estate is a nearly ideal investment during inflation, but its very strengths turn into weaknesses during a negative sum investing game.

Real estate uses debt—the more the better. Paying off that debt with a 30-year fixed rate mortgage is a blessing if inflation makes that debt vastly cheaper in real terms. (At 10 percent inflation for 30 years, a dollar of debt loses 95 percent of its real value.) There is no blessing at all, however, if the mortgage carries a high rate of interest and then inflation disappears in a depression.

The reasons that real estate declines in value start with the reasons that drove it up. Real estate is such a good inflation hedge that many properties are driven up in price so high that they no longer produce a positive cash flow (i.e., the rental income from the property is insufficient to cover operating payments and mortgage service). Buyers of these properties are willing to accept negative cash flows because they make at least one of two optimistic assumptions:

1. They will be able to raise rents enough to produce a positive cash flow.

2. The price of the property will continue to go up. This is the "greater-fool" theory which counts on the continuing willingness of speculators to buy at ever-higher prices. The danger is that the investor will turn out to be the greatest fool of all.

Both those happy assumptions are demolished in a negative sum investing game. Landlords are likely to be unable to raise rents in an economy with no inflation. Worse yet, they may find their rents going down instead of up. Workers who lose their jobs will be unable to pay rent on their apartments, so a landlord will find vacancies, evictions, and bad debts all going up at the same time. As businesses go bankrupt, they will be less able to pay rent to the owners of office buildings and shopping centers. Most property buyers assume their properties will produce ever-increasing income, but flat or declining income can be a disaster when combined with high fixed costs (e.g., mortgage service, utilities, property management) and an initial negative cash flow.

The initial negative cash flow, which the investor thought would be temporary, now becomes reasonably permanent. Since a permanent negative cash flow is a good prescription for personal bankruptcy, the investor's next thought is to sell the property for at least what was paid for it. Maybe the investor will be lucky enough to find another naive and greedy buyer, but more likely there will be many other desperate sellers competing to unload their own properties. To sell the property, the seller will have to lower its price to the point where the cash flow is both positive and high enough to induce one of the few scarce buyers to purchase it. Lowering the price of leveraged property will reduce or erase the seller's equity. If the investor put up 20 percent of the property's price and borrowed the remaining 80 percent, then even a 10 percent decline in the price of the property will wipe out half ($10 \div 20$) of the investor's equity.

## WHEN EVERYTHING WENT WRONG

Declining property prices were a painful reality during the depression of the 1930s. Homeowners lost their homes when they lost their jobs and became unable to meet their mortgage payments. Owners of income-producing property saw their incomes decline while their mortgage costs remained fixed. Farmers who spent the late 1920s in their own private depression resorted to an interesting strategy to retain their lands. When a bankrupt farmer's property was sold in foreclosure, the neighbors showed up with an ample supply of guns. While the neighbors discouraged other potential bidders, the desperate farmer made an extremely low bid for the old farm. Bankers quickly caught on to these "penny auctions," but the need of farmers to try such a desperate ploy demonstrated just how bad the situation for landowners was.

A more recent example of property owners in trouble took place in California during the early 1980s. Home prices boomed there in the inflation of the late 1970s, sending the average home price well over $100,000 and well beyond the average homeowner's ability to afford one. Conventional lenders conveniently relaxed their formerly conser vative credit limits, and when those newly liberalized limits were reached, sellers transformed themselves into lenders to keep the boom going. Other parts of the country also enjoyed rising home prices, but California stood out as the worst example of speculative excess.

What goes up so far frequently comes down so hard, as California home prices proved in the early 1980s. Everything went wrong at once:

Interest rates soared as high as 17 percent for first mortgages and even higher for second mortgages. Even more significant than the remarkably high level of nominal mortgage rates was the even higher level of real mortgage rates. Since home prices began going down instead of up, the real mortgage rate (i.e., the nominal interest rate less the gain in the price of the home) was more than the nominal rate of 17 percent.

The "balloons" of seller financing began to burst in late 1982. Many homes in the late 1970s were financed with notes taken back from sellers at 10 percent interest which called for balloon payments due in 3 to 5 years. Buyers assumed they would be able to refinance at lower rates when the balloon payments came due, but found to their dismay that second mortgage rates were far higher instead. *A basic principle of sound finance is to match the maturities of assets and liabilities,* but many buyers violated that principle by using a short-term liability (i.e., a 3- to 5-year note from the seller) to finance the long-term asset of a home.

Savings and loan associations, the major providers of housing finance, got into trouble by mismatching their maturities too. They used short-term assets in the form of savers' deposits to make long-term mortgage loans. When the interest rate on deposits rose above relatively fixed rates on mortgages, savings and loans were plunged into losses which amounted to 2 percent of their net worth per month. Confronted by a shrinking equity base, savings and loans shrank their new mortgage originations to a fraction of their previous levels. Since real estate prices depend heavily on the flow of credit (or lack of it), the crippling of the major source of real estate credit was a heavy blow to homeowners.

An estimated 80 percent of home purchases involved seller financing, and most of those involved the assumption of an old, low-rate first or second mortgage. In the *Wellenkamp* decision, California courts voided the "due-on-sale" clauses in mortgages which would have permitted lenders to escape from their old below-market-rate mortgages whenever a home was sold. In 1982 the U.S. Supreme Court upheld "due-on-sale" clauses and thereby enabled savings and loans to call in mortgages where the home had been sold. For buyers who assumed a 7 percent mortgage and later discovered that they had to replace it with another mortgage at perhaps twice the old interest rate, the "due-on-sale" decision by the U.S. Supreme Court was a very expensive change in the rules of the financing game.

Home prices declined at least 10 percent between 1979 and 1982 when allowing for the effects of seller financing at concessionary rates; but that figure is only a rough estimate, because there is no reliable guide to average real estate prices which corresponds to the Dow Jones industrial average for stocks. Since general inflation moved up while home prices declined, buyers found that a home was no longer a great investment but simply a nice place to live.

Rental prices moved up far more slowly than purchase prices during the 1970s. As a result, virtually no home bought in the late 1970s generated enough rent to pay for maintenance, taxes, and mortgage service. Buyers who tried to rent their speculatively purchased homes found that they had large negative cash flows. That left them two unpleasant alternatives: continue to rent the home and accept the negative cash flow or sell the home in a depressed market and take a loss.

## SOME REAL ESTATE WILL BENEFIT

Not all real estate is likely to suffer equally in a negative sum investing game. The worst loser will be the last buyer of a high-priced apartment building with a negative cash flow and a double-digit mortgage. Other major losers include property still in the construction stage, because it generates no income and may not be marketable when it is finished. Any property whose income is vulnerable to decrease will be in danger.

Other properties will fare much better. An office building whose income is secured by long-term leases with financially strong tenants may come through unscathed. A shopping center with solid tenants may suffer little loss of current income even though its prospective income from percentage rents may decline. (Most shopping centers collect part of their rent in the form of a percentage of their tenants'

sales. These percentage rents will rise only as long as tenants' sales do.)
A few properties will show actual increases in value *late* in a negative sum investing game if they are fortunate enough to have very stable incomes. Capitalization rates, which vary inversely with values, are likely to decline as the depression really takes hold and inflation declines. The accompanying table shows the values for the same property based on two different capitalization rates.

|  | Inflationary economy | Noninflationary economy |
| --- | --- | --- |
| Income | $1 million | $1 million |
| Capitalization rate | 10 percent | 5 percent |
| Value (income ÷ capitalization rate) | $10 million | $20 million |

## THE DEBACLE OF REITs

The debacle of the real estate investment trusts (REITs) in the mid 1970s is worth a separate note. An REIT is the real estate equivalent of a mutual fund which allows investors to pool their funds in a diversified portfolio of properties and mortgages. Most REITs were founded together in the mid 1970s, and many of them floundered together a few years later. The causes of the REITs' disaster offer an insight as to what can go wrong in real estate:

The worst losses were taken by REITs which specialized in short-term construction and land development projects, neither of which produced any current income. When the recession of 1973 to 1975 hit, many of these properties were not completed or could not find buyers when they were completed. Financing properties that produced no income with debt tied to the soaring prime rate caused negative cash flows which bankrupted developers and REITs alike.

The virtues of professional management were vastly overpromoted to the public. One professionally managed REIT even managed to have every one of its loans in default at the same time. In real estate as in other areas of investing, the experts are most likely to be wrong when they are most unanimously in agreement.

The illiquidity of real estate was a problem both on the way up and on the way down. As the burgeoning REITs took in large amounts of money, they competed for a limited number of good projects and drove their prices up. When they later foreclosed on projects in default and tried to sell them, they found few buyers and many other REITs competing to sell similarly distressed properties.

Two classes of investors made good money in REITs. Those who bought early before REITs were popular enjoyed some gains if they sold them after the bandwagon was rolling. Investors who waited until the prices of REITs went off a cliff made money through the distress of the majority of investors who bought into REITs when they were popular.

Special-purpose funds—in this case real estate—generally come out in large numbers when that special purpose is near the peak of its popularity and price. Generally an investor is better off avoiding such special-purpose funds until after a shakeout has taken place. Other examples of special-purpose funds include energy, precious metals, and private placements.

# THE LOSERS—PRECIOUS METALS

Gold is a sterile asset. It produces no goods or services and it costs money to store and insure.

All that makes no difference during inflation because increases in the price of gold more than offset its disadvantages. Without inflation to drive up its price, however, gold is a dead weight for investors. Even if gold does not decline in price (it dropped from $850 per ounce to $300 per ounce in the 3 years up to 1982), it is distinctly unprofitable compared with better alternatives.

Gold is a hedge against political instability as well as a hedge against inflation. Because it is small relative to its value, gold is easily concealed from tax collectors, revolutionaries, and invading armies. For centuries the French—whose experience with inflation, war, and revolution has been both frequent and unhappy—have been premier hoarders of gold.

Valuing gold is extraordinarily difficult. It has neither profits nor dividends, so there is no way to value it on the basis of a price/earnings ratio or current yield. Its value in time of political instability is high, but translating that value into a precise number of dollars is impossible.

Gold also has uses as jewelry and in electronics, both of which are quite sensitive to price. The net result is that the value of gold is subject to a large amount of necessary imprecision and usually unproven opinion.

Like gold, silver has industrial uses, particularly in photography. Unlike gold, industrial uses largely determine silver's price because it is no longer used as money or currency reserves by most of the world's central banks. Silver's price is likely to rise during inflation along with the prices of other commodities and to fall during recessions or depression along with the prices of other commodities. The Hunt brothers tried to corner the market in silver and lost over $1 billion because even their extensive financial resources were insufficient to prevent its price from going down.

Diamonds are a very different store of value. When the New York Stock Exchange lost its power to control brokerage rates on May Day 1975, the mantle of the world's oldest and most successful price-fixing monopoly passed to DeBeers Consolidated Mines. Ever since Cecil John Rhodes formed a marketing cartel in diamonds at the turn of the century, DeBeers has been an extraordinarily efficient monopoly by following three strategies:

1. Since diamonds have no intrinsic value except as abrasives (unlike oil and other objects of monopoly activity), DeBeers has employed an enormously successful long-term advertising campaign to create demand by convincing women (and therefore men) of the world that those tiny sparkling stones are tangible symbols of love and worth. Even in Japan, DeBeers's tasteful advertising has convinced women that diamonds are for engagements and other special occasions. Unlike the victims of monopoly pricing in other goods and services, women have a vested interest in maintaining the cartel because if it cracked and diamond prices fell, few women would enjoy recognizing that their previously valuable symbol of love was just a worthless sparkling little stone.

2. To maintain price stability, DeBeers stockpiles diamonds during periods of slack demand and then sells its stockpile as world demand improves.

3. When faced with potential competition from a new source of supply, DeBeers coopts the competition. Even the Soviet Union, no friend of monopoly capitalism or apartheid (DeBeers is based in South Africa), cooperates in marketing its diamonds through the cartel. When the Soviets began to produce more small stones in the mid 1970s, DeBeers created the eternity ring as an innovative way to market them. The recent discovery of huge diamond deposits in Australia posed a threat to the cartel, but DeBeers quickly reached an agreement to market

most of those gemstones. Zaire left the diamond cartel partially for political reasons, but economic pressure forced it to return to the fold in 1983. Most diamond producers cooperate with DeBeers because it is in every producer's interest to keep this very profitable cartel going.

In theory, DeBeers's control of diamond prices should place a floor under diamond prices for investors. In practice, it does not work nearly that neatly. DeBeers discourages speculation in diamonds and, in a powerful display of monopoly power in action, bankrupted many diamond cutters who participated in a flurry of speculation in 1978 and 1979. For all its power, however, DeBeers is far from omnipotent; in the early 1980s the world economic contraction was the most difficult challenge to its existence since the 1930s. A 1-carat D-flawless diamond, the speculator's benchmark, fell from $60,000 to under $20,000 in less than 3 years.

Even if diamonds did have a stable floor, they would have several drawbacks for investors. They are not uniform in size, shape, color, flaws, fluorescence, etc., and even experts differ by wide margins about the value of any particular stone. (By contrast, gold comes in uniform ounces.) There is a large dealer markup amounting to as much as 50 percent of stones bought "wholesale." It takes a great deal of price appreciation just to recoup the dealer's large profit.

## THE LOSERS—ANTIQUES AND OTHER COLLECTIBLES

Old masters and old English shotguns share a common problem with gold. They produce no income (apart from aesthetic pleasure and grouse on the table), so they are worth only what someone else will pay. When money is loose in an inflationary environment, people are willing to pay far more than when money is tight in a recession or depression.

Collectibles also share some problems with diamonds. They are not uniform (one Picasso painting may be worth far more than another), and even experts may differ widely on their values. When an investor buys or sells, the dealer or auction house imposes a stiff toll charge to cover its expenses and profit.

Collectibles also have problems all their own. They are subject to fads which can lower or raise their value, independent of inflation. The fact that one school of artists strikes the collective fancy of art collectors today does not necessarily mean that anyone will care in 5 years when another school is in vogue. Even in the best of times, collectibles are illiquid. In the worst of times, the investor is likely to be stuck with a declining asset and no place to sell it.

Money can be made in collectibles, but generally only by patient investors who take the time to understand the market for their specialty. For investors with enough time and money, the best policy is to build collections of things they like and know well. If they make a profit, then they are even farther ahead, and at least they are assured of something they can enjoy in the meantime.

## THE LOSERS—COMMON STOCKS

Profits decline in depressions; for some companies profits turn into large losses. In a financial version of Newtonian mechanics, the companies whose profits go up most when the economy is expanding generally see those profits decline most when it is contracting. The most vulnerable companies have at least some of the following characteristics:

High operating leverage (e.g., the steel, aluminum, paper, auto, and airline industries).

High financial leverage with large amounts of debt.

New and unseasoned policies and personnel, especially if they are in industries with rapidly changing technology.

Production of commodities.

Marginal profitability even in good times. These lame ducks become sitting ducks when the economy contracts.

A serious recession brings out a seldom-noticed fact about common stock: it represents a residual claim on earnings. Stockholders get the lion's share of rising profits when business is good, but they are the first to suffer when business turns sour. Stockholders are last in line behind employees, suppliers, and creditors.

Stockholders are also last in line to claim the company's assets in case of bankruptcy. There is an adage that a company's liabilities are always good; it is the assets which are of doubtful value. After a bankrupt company's assets are paid out to everyone else, there may be little left for stockholders.

While most stocks will decline in a depression, a few actually go up, as with properties. There will be a few companies with unusually stable sources of income (high-quality utilities, foods, and tobaccos are likely candidates) which may come through with their profits relatively unscathed. The price/earnings ratios which the market applies to those profits are likely to go up as interest rates and inflation come down *late* in a depression. If a company can maintain its profits at $5 per share while P/E ratios go from 8 to 12, then its stock price will rise from $40 to $60.

While depression is a major influence on stock prices, it is not the only one. The absence or presence of speculative frenzy also has a large role in determining how far stocks will fall. One reason the stock market fell so far (89 percent) in 1929 to 1932 is that the decline began from a high level of speculation which bid prices up to extraordinary heights. A similar decline is unlikely today because the stock market as a whole has been a disappointment to investors since the 1960s; the Dow Jones industrial average spent most of 1982 in the 800 to 1000 range, which is also where it spent most of 1966.

Since stock prices generally anticipate economic events, they are likely to rise well before a depression hits bottom. Stock prices reached their lowest level in 1932, while the economy bottomed in 1933 and stayed down for most of the rest of the decade. The tendency of stocks to be a leading indicator of the economy (see Chapter 1) means that they are likely to be the first major losers even before the economy plunges, but also are likely to be the first winners when a recession or depression is obviously under way. Just as the stock market bottomed in 1932, well before the economy hit its low in 1933, the stock market may have bottomed in August of 1982, well before the controlled depression ended.

# THE WINNERS—BONDS

Every fruit has its season. For bonds that season is the negative sum investing game. They are a poor investment in a positive sum game and a terrible investment in a zero sum one. Their strengths come out only in times of adversity.

Bonds are *guaranteed* as to the payments of principal and interest. No such guarantees exist for shareholders who stand last in line in their claim on profits. Last in line is the worst place to be when profits decline in a nasty depression. Bondholders are at the head of the line (along with bankers), so their income is far more assured.

Bondholders will enjoy a *positive* real rate of return, in contrast to the negative real returns which penalize them in an inflationary economy. The holder of a 10 percent bond receives a 0 percent real return at 10 percent inflation, a 5 percent real return at 5 percent inflation, and a 10 percent real return at zero inflation. Declining inflation combines with fixed principal and interest payments to create rising real returns for investors.

Bonds are likely to produce capital gains in addition to good current real returns. In the latter part of a depression, interest rates will decline along with inflation, causing bond prices to rise. Bonds will be one of the few investments which rise in value during a negative sum investing game. The accompanying table shows the real returns on bonds in positive, zero, and negative sum economies under GNP deflator and real GNP growth rates.

Bond quality is not very important during positive and zero sum investing games. There are few defaults, and quality spreads (the difference in yield between high-quality bonds and low-quality ones) are generally excessive. In a negative sum investing game, however, quality is much more important. Defaults and credit downgradings are likely to be far more frequent than investors expect, so the best policy is to stick to high-quality bonds such as government-guaranteed issues (e.g., Treasury obligations and government national mortgage association

| | GNP deflator, % | | |
|---|---|---|---|
| | Less than 0 | 0 to 2.99 | 3.00 or over |
| Real interest rates for long-term, high-grade corporate bonds, 1900–1981 | 7.7 percent | 2.0 percent | –2.0 percent |
| Number of years | 17 | 28 | 36 |
| | Real GNP growth rates, % | | |
| | Less than 0 | 0 to 2.99 | 3.00 or over |
| Real interest rates for long-term, high-grade corporate bonds, 1900–1981 | 2.6 percent | 1.0 percent | 1.0 percent |
| Number of years | 23 | 15 | 43 |

*Source:* Salomon Bros., Henry Kaufman Pamphlet; Why Interest Rates Are So High; May 20, 1982.

certificates). Some high-quality corporate bonds will offer slightly higher returns to investors who are willing and able to do their own credit research. The much higher returns available in low-quality bonds are little advantage if the company which issued them goes bankrupt. Low-quality bonds generally are defined as ones with a Baa or lower rating by Moody or Standard and Poor.

*After* a company goes bankrupt, its bonds may offer excellent value. Bonds in bankrupt companies frequently sell for 30 to 40 cents on the dollar and offer excellent potential for income and capital gains. There is a large risk, however, that an investor without the necessary time and expertise will get stuck with bonds which later become worthless, and will pay large commissions to do it.

Even high-quality bonds with negligible credit risk have a large amount of interest-rate risk attached to them. Interest rates are generally volatile during a zero sum investing game (they became much more volatile after the Federal Reserve began its new operating policy in October 1979) and during the early stages of a negative sum investing game. Volatile interest rates mean that only investors who can live with widely fluctuating bond prices should buy the longer-dated maturities where the fluctuations are greatest. Three rules of thumb are useful for bond investors:

1. Buy bonds only after a recession or depression is clearly under way.
2. Buy bonds only when their yield is at least 5 percent above the last 12 months of inflation. The danger that inflation and interest rates will rise again is the major risk facing bondholders, so they should not put their money at risk unless they are being well paid to take it.
3. Buy only bonds with a large amount of call protection to ensure that a decline in interest rates translates into a corresponding rise in the prices of the investor's bonds. Call protection may be obtained by using Treasury bonds or low-coupon corporate bonds which are selling well below par.

# THE WINNERS—CASH EQUIVALENTS

Like bonds, cash is a good investment only in a negative sum investing game. In addition to positive real returns, high-quality cash equivalents offer freedom from loss and the opportunity to buy other investments at lower prices.

Rising returns go to scarce commodities, and cash is the scarce commodity in a negative sum investing game. The demand for cash goes up as business people and speculators who ran down their balance sheets to capitalize on earlier inflation suddenly switch to repairing those balance sheets to protect against depression. The supply of funds is limited by the Federal Reserve's attempt to fight against inflation. Rising demand and constricting supply add up to rising returns on cash equivalents. Even better, rising returns on cash equivalents combine with receding inflation to produce large *real* returns for investors. The generous real returns on cash equivalents look even better still when compared with the declining real and nominal returns on other assets.

Declining prices on other assets give the holders of cash the *opportunity* to pick up bargains. The investor with speculative assets supported by large debts will be in too much trouble to capitalize on declines in the prices of those assets. As speculators in trouble are forced to sell their assets at distress prices to pay their debts, the investor with cash will have the opportunity to buy them cheaply.

Not all cash equivalents are created equal. Treasury bills are riskless, and the obligations of federal agencies (e.g., Federal Farm Credit, Federal Home Loan Bank) are virtually so. Federally insured accounts at banks and savings and loan associations also qualify as virtually riskless. Money market mutual funds which invest in federal obligations qualify as virtually riskless too. However, most money market mutual funds invest not only in federal obligations, but also in the commercial paper of major corporations and in certificates of deposits and acceptances of major banks. Generally those nonfederal obligations are high-quality, low-risk assets which yield more than assets with a federal guarantee. As a depression deepens, however, the investor is better off remaining in federally guaranteed assets to protect against the small chance of a large loss.

The real returns on cash equivalents were marginal at best until the late 1970s. At that time two major and related secular changes took place to benefit investors.

The Federal Reserve began its new policy of practical monetarism in October of 1979. The new policy was to shift from controlling interest rates (in practice that meant controlling them at an artificially low level) to controlling the growth of the money supply. When the Fed took its lid off interest rates, they promptly went up to all-time record levels. The demand for money does not respond to small changes in interest rates, so the Fed had to allow large and generally upward changes in them to achieve its monetary targets. Despite the Fed's shift away from practical monetarism and toward stimulation in October 1982, real interest rates remained notably positive. The genie of positive real interest rates, once out of the bottle, seems difficult to put back inside.

Even if the Fed becomes a total apostate to its new religion of practical monetarism, the deregulation of interest rates will act to raise the real return on cash equivalents in the 1980s. For decades federal regulations limited the interest rates the nation's depositors could receive on their checking and savings accounts to low or negative levels in real terms. As market rates of interest soared in the 1970s, so did the growth of mutual funds offering those market rates along with check-writing privileges. By 1982 money market funds had accumulated $230 billion, or roughly half of the amount remaining in banks and savings and loans in the form of deposits bearing interest rates of 5 percent or less. Prodded by the competition and permitted by Congress, which moved to deregulate interest rates, reluctant bankers began to offer market rates to their customers. Deregulation of interest rates and increased competition among the providers of financial services benefit precisely the party which economic theory says they should benefit—the nation's depositors. Even if the Fed totally abandons practical monetarism, the secular change toward free-market interest rates should help maintain positive real rates of interest on cash equivalents.

Cash and bonds are clear winners in a negative sum investing game. Common stocks with stable earnings may be winners if purchased at distress prices, as the depression deepens. High-quality real estate with stable income also may benefit. High-quality and assured income characterize the winning assets in a negative sum investing game.

# CHAPTER FOUR

# THE ZERO SUM ECONOMY

A zero sum economy is not always an inflationary one. Before the industrial revolution in Britain, most of humankind existed in a steady state economy which changed little from one generation to the next in terms of prices and output. An occasional war, plague, or bad harvest might lower living standards, but in general the young could see a good preview of their own lives in the lives their parents and grandparents led. In this kind of stable society there were three principal routes to wealth: inherit it, marry it, or steal it.

A fourth route to wealth has been added to the other three: capitalize on inflation. Rising prices create a massive redistribution of income and wealth. The economy is like a giant poker game where there is a loser for every winner. What separates the winners from the losers is their ability to understand inflation and to turn it to their advantage.

An economy can be a zero sum one from an investor's perspective even if some real growth is still present. If secular real growth in the economy is only 1 to 2 percent and secular inflation is about 10 percent, then real growth simply does not count. What counts for investors is the big numbers in the economy, and the big numbers came from inflation in the United States starting in 1973. In practice, real growth seldom maintains its previous upward course once inflation grips the economy.

# THE FINANCIAL CAUSES OF INFLATION—THE PAPER ECONOMY

A good prescription for terminal boredom is a technical description of the monetary system and its components. To avoid this tendency toward boredom as much as possible, the following description of the financial causes of inflation uses a minimum of numbers and technical terms. Even well-informed readers are encouraged not to skip this section, because its treatment of the financial causes of inflation is quite different from the traditional approach.

Too much money is a necessary condition of inflation. Every nation which has experienced a sustained increase in its general price level also has experienced an increase in the amount of money in circulation. Political demagogues may gain votes by blaming OPEC, greedy oil companies, socially unresponsive unions, etc., but the pricipal cause of inflation is irresponsible politicians who print too much money. Occasionally one powerful group may boost the prices of its product faster than others (e.g., OPEC in 1973), but only an increase in the money supply will push up the general price level in the economy as a whole.

Blaming inflation on money supply growth is correct as far as it goes, but it does not go far enough in explaining the financial causes of inflation. The broader financial causes of inflation involve a broader concept which, for lack of any other accepted name, may be called the *paper economy.*

Alongside the physical economy, which produces real goods and services, there is a paper economy, which produces claims on those goods and services. The paper economy exists on three levels, all of which ultimately interact with each other to produce inflation: money, credit, and pensions and entitlements.

## THE FIRST LEVEL—THE MONEY SUPPLY

The money supply is the first level of the paper economy. Currently popular definitions of the money supply include cash, checking accounts, NOW (negotiable order of withdrawal) accounts, savings accounts, and at least some portion of money market funds. The common characteristic of all these definitions of money is that they all can be used for *transactions* purposes. Cash pays for groceries at the corner supermarket. A check or draft on a NOW account pays the rent. Money market funds are not pure transactions balances (there is some savings component as well), but their check-writing features put them close enough to other transactions balances to include them in conventional definitions of money.

The monetarist school of economics places great emphasis on controlling the money supply as a way to control inflation. They change their operating definition of the money supply from time to time, but transactions balances are the real focus of their theories and policy recommendations. From the perspective of the paper economy, however, the money supply is only the tip of the iceberg.

## THE SECOND LEVEL—CREDIT

The bulk of the iceberg consists of credit. Credit is someone's promise to pay money at some future date; technically it is a liability. Examples of credit instruments include bonds, mortgages, commercial paper, Treasury notes and bills, and certificates of deposit. The total amount of credit instruments is many times larger than the money supply.

The traditional distinction between money and credit is that credit can't be used for transactions. No one pays for groceries with a 2-year Treasury note for $100,000. No one pays for rent with a $500,000 bank certificate of deposit due in 6 months. Credit may be viewed as "future money" which is not spendable now. In economic terms, credit instruments generally represent the savings of someone looking for a store of value.

The distinction between money and credit matters a great deal in an economy without efficient capital markets. If the central bank wants to reduce inflation, it sells long-term bonds in return for money held by its citizens. The withdrawal of money from circulation reduces the amount of money consumers have available to spend. Reduced spending means reduced inflationary pressure. An increase in the velocity of money (i.e., the speed with which a dollar changes hands in a year) can offset a decrease in the amount of money in the hands of the public, but the usual outcome is that the sale of Treasury securities mops up excess purchasing power and thereby curtails inflation.

It all seems so neat at first, but the distinction between money and credit falls apart in an economy with efficient capital markets. When the central bank sells Treasury bonds to the public in exchange for money, the result is only a brief withdrawal of purchasing power. Whenever the holders of 2-year $100,000 Treasury notes want to spend them, they simply go to their local brokers, who sell the notes for them and give them money in return. The nation's capital markets are really a giant vehicle for transforming credit into money and back again. Even low-quality credit instruments such as second trust deeds can be sold in return for cash.

The presence of an efficient capital market (U.S. capital markets are very efficient) simply destroys the traditional distinction between money and credit. If money and credit can be changed into each other quickly and efficiently, then they are practically identical from the perspective of controlling inflation. No one pays rent with a $500,000 bank certificate of deposit due in 6 months, but the holder can transform a CD into rent money by selling it through the medium of the nation's capital markets.

One form of credit does not require the capital markets to convert it into money. Unused lines of credit for consumers and business people are treated by the public as money even though they are not counted as such. The consumer with a $5000 line of credit on a VISA card uses that in lieu of money to buy meals, stereos, plane tickets, etc. The business person with a $100 million line of credit from the bank rightly considers it as money. It can be used to pay a supplier, build a factory, buy more inventory, or acquire a corporation. A line of credit technically does not become part of the money supply until it is converted into a loan, but both consumers and business people rightly regard it as highly liquid money immediately available to finance transactions.

Viewing money and credit as practically identical is more than an academic exercise; it leads to conclusions very different from those offered by the monetarist school of economics. The monetarists' policy prescription of controlling the money supply is unlikely to be effective in controlling inflation unless credit expansion also is controlled. The Federal Reserve has extensive legal power to impose credit controls, but it seldom uses that power. When the Fed did use credit controls briefly in early 1980, the result was a sharp drop in economic activity, demonstrating that they can be powerful when used. Normally, however, there is no effective control on the expansion of credit which frequently offsets the Fed's attempts to slow the expansion of the money supply. As long as abundant credit is available to finance economic activity (including inflation), the monetarist attempt to reduce money supply growth is likely to be ineffective in promoting stable prices.

Viewing money and credit as practically identical leads to very different conclusions about interest rates, a subject of major concern to investors. The explosion of interest rates in 1980 and 1981 came as a surprise to most government and academic economists who concentrated on the wiggles of money supply growth. Virtually the only ones to predict the new peaks in interest rates were a few economists employed by Wall Street brokerage firms, such as Henry Kaufman at Salomon Brothers. Their practical experience in transforming money into a credit and back again gave them an advantage other economists did not have. They saw that the credit demands of an expanding private sector would collide with the deficit-fueled credit demands of the federal government. Even higher interest rates were the result of that collision.

## THE THIRD LEVEL—PENSIONS, ENTITLEMENTS, AND FOREIGN CLAIMS

Combining money and credit produces both a more accurate picture of the inflationary forces in the economy and a more accurate forecast of interest rates. That is not, however, the outer limit of the paper economy. Unfunded pension claims, including Social Security entitlements and foreign claims against the U.S. dollar also are components of the paper economy.

At first there seems no connection between today's inflation and a worker's pension right or Social Security entitlement due in 20 years. The pension right cannot be spent at the local supermarket and cannot be converted into money through the medium of the nation's capital markets. Despite its lack of liquidity, that distant pension claim has both short-term and long-term inflationary impact.

The short-term inflationary impact of a distant pension claim arises from the worker's diminished need to save for retirement. In the bad old days before Social Security and generous company pensions, workers had to save a large portion of their incomes to support themselves in old age.[1] Now workers feel free to save less and spend more under the comfortable assumption that Uncle Sam and their former employer will take care of them. This "spend it now" attitude adds more demand to an economy already under pressure from demand-induced inflation. The reduced savings lowers the amount of capital available to support investment and future economic growth which will pay for future pensions. In monetarist terms, the prospect of generous future pensions converts the worker's money from savings balances seeking a store of value to transactions balances available for immediate spending.

The short-term inflationary impact of workers' diminished need to save for retirement pales beside the long-term impact of unfunded pension claims. Except for a few highly publicized exceptions, the pri-

---

[1] In Japan the workers still do need to save for their retirement because their pension plans are not very generous, which is one reason Japan's personal savings rate is so much higher than our own.

vate pension system is on the whole reasonably well funded. Total unfunded pensions in the private sector run only into billions, far below the trillions in unfunded entitlements at the federal, state, and local levels. At all levels, governments in this country have promised pensions, medical and disability payments, and other forms of relief whose present value is far beyond the value of assets in the funds set aside to pay them.

These unfunded government entitlements are the legacy of members of the "spend and elect" school of politics, many of whom are still members of Congress. They bought votes in the 1960s and 1970s by generously passing out future medical and pension entitlements. It all seemed so painless at the time, because passing out future entitlements did nothing to increase the federal deficit in the year the votes were bought.

Yesterday's painless purchase of votes is now today's bloated budget deficit. Each passing year of the 1980s and 1990s will bring the bills due for the entitlements so freely passed out during the 1960s and 1970s. The narcotic growth of entitlement payments propels government spending upward without any matching increase in government revenues. President Carter believed he had fixed the Social Security system for at least a decade, but it was in trouble again within a year of his leaving office. That trouble translates into ever-expanding budget deficits which have only two unpalatable solutions: unpopular increases in taxes or unpopular cuts in entitlements.

The impact of entitlements on government budgets illustrates the essential unity of the paper economy. Future entitlements in time became current expenditures, leading to yawning government deficits. Those federal deficits are financed in one of two ways: printing money or issuing new Treasury securities. Printing new money is directly inflationary. New Treasury securities are inflationary with a lag; the lag can be as short as the few days it takes for the buyer to transform them into cash through the medium of the nation's capital markets.

Both credit instruments and pension entitlements are "future money" which cannot be spent now but which may be spent later. The willingness of investors to hold their assets in "future money" depends upon their confidence in the future value of that money and upon how much they are being paid to wait until the future arrives. As inflation goes from the exceptional case to the accepted norm, confidence in the value of "future money" rapidly disappears. As confidence in the future value of money declines, the interest rate must go up to pay investors to take the risk of losing the real value of their assets to inflation. Once inflation is deeply embedded, as in the early 1980s, interest rates often rise to very high levels in both nominal and real (i.e., nominal interest less inflation) terms to compensate for the risk that inflation will accelerate to new heights. Unfortunately, high real rates of interest are likely to precipitate a depression which undermines the physical economy's ability to produce goods and services to meet its credit obligations and future pension needs.

If the U.S. economy were isolated, money, credit, pensions, and entitlements would be the only major components of the paper economy. Since the U.S. economy is open to the rest of the world, the rest of the world has claims on the U.S. economy. The Eurodollar market has been a large but misunderstood source of increase in the paper economy. From almost nothing 15 years ago, this pool of stateless money has grown to about $1.3 trillion at the end of 1981, or roughly one-third of current U.S. GNP. The prospect that foreigners might present all those dollar claims at once is the stuff of novels about financial catastrophe and hyperinflation.

In fact most of those dollars outside the United States are likely to stay there. The U.S. dollar is the principal currency of international trade, and many of those Eurodollars finance trade which has nothing to do with spending in the U.S. economy. Since a large but unknown portion of the Eurodollar market consists of interbank deposits, the net amount of real spending power is less than appears on the surface. In addition, some portion of the Eurodollar market consists of anonymous wealth seeking a long-term store of value (that is also true for U.S. government securities held by OPEC nations), which is highly unlikely to be spent on today's goods and services.

Even with the above conditions, the Eurodollar market still presents two very real dangers. It is an uncontrolled source of new paper claims on goods and services which adds to worldwide inflation. The fact that it is uncontrolled sets the stage for a financial crisis of the kind described in Chapter 2.

Merely because an activity can be identified does not mean there is anyone in charge of it or able to control it. When the Federal Reserve tries to control some element of the paper economy such as the domestic money supply, growth is likely to pick up in other areas such as commercial paper and Eurodollar loans. The Fed has no control over the deficits created by Congress, and, in practice, neither do members of Congress; much of the current federal spending is in "uncontrollable" items such as entitlements which usually are the present result of past congressional generosity. The paper economy is a juggernaut which took many years to start growing, but now is extraordinarily hard to stop. Until the uncontrolled growth of the paper economy is halted, no permanent halt to inflation is possible either.

# THE FISCAL CAUSES OF
# INFLATION

The fiscal causes of inflation are disarmingly simple. The government runs large deficits which stimulate demand. Stimulating demand for goods and services beyond the economy's ability to supply them generates inflation.

A balanced budget once was considered a basic principle of sound public finance.[2] Both Herbert Hoover and Franklin Roosevelt promised balanced budgets, as was the custom in their time. Deficits were a vice until the Keynesians made them virtues. The virtues of deficits included their ability to stimulate the economy out of recession and into expansionary paradise.

Politicians saw another virtue to deficits. Ever since the "bread and circuses" days of the late Roman Empire, politicians have pandered for votes by spending the public's purse on what the voters wanted. In modern times this came to be known as the "spend and elect" school of politics, which found its home in the Democratic party. The Democrats spent heavily on their supporters to ensure their continued support. When the constraint of a balanced budget was removed by public acceptance of perpetual deficits, the Democrats joyfully discovered that they could spend even more to buy votes.

The Republicans, whose folklore includes the image of fiscal rectitude, behaved no better once in office. Except for one year under President Nixon, the federal budget has not been balanced for nearly a generation. The difference between the Democrats and the Republicans is not their propensity to bust the budget with deficits, since both parties do so with equal abandon. The difference is who benefits from the extra spending which causes the deficit. President Reagan illustrated this principle by reducing the increases of spending on "liberal" programs such as welfare and shifting it to "conservative" programs such as defense and tax cuts for the wealthy. Both presidents Carter and Reagan firmly promised balanced budgets at the end of their 4 years in office; Carter calmly broke that promise (among many others), and Reagan seems likely to do the same unless there is a drastic change in current projections for federal taxes and expenditures.

Despite the tendency of both parties to incur deficits, the Democrats clearly enjoy it more. Liberal Democratic dogma suggests that spending on liberal causes is so virtuous that fiscal vices don't count. The

---

[2]From 1791 to 1983, there were 101 years of surplus and 92 years of deficit.

Republicans approach massive deficits with ambivalence; their morals do not prevent them from committing the act, only from deriving any pleasure from it.

Humans are not just rational animals; they are rationalizing ones. Having selected a position for whatever reason, they then rationalize an elaborate justification for it. The justification which Keynesians developed for continuing massive deficits was the need to stimulate the economy out of depression. Once created, those massive deficits developed powerful constituencies which powerfully opposed any cut in their benefits.

Large as it is, the federal deficit does not measure the total impact of the federal government. Off-budget agencies borrow money for farmers (Federal Farm Credit) and homeowners (Federal Home Loan Bank), and they guarantee loans to troubled companies such as Chrysler. A good rule of thumb is that the federal deficit seriously understates the size and nature of the government's impact on today's inflationary economy.

While both Democrats and Republicans ran large deficits justified by Keynesian logic, it was the Democrats who became natural allies of Keynesian economists. The Democrats were in search of an intellectual justification for their spend and elect approach to liberalism. The Keynesians were academics in search of recognition, influence, and political power. Liberal Democrats and Keynesians together enjoyed a symbiosis which propelled them into their zenith of power, recognition, and honor in 1969, and into increasing obscurity subsequently.

Statistically, the nexus between federal deficits and inflation is more difficult to pin down than might be expected. Deficits currently run about 3 percent of GNP[3] (more in recessionary years, less in expansionary ones), so the influences of the other 97 percent of the economy tend to be far more powerful over short periods of time. Separating that 3 percent from the rest of the effects of business cycles, oil embargoes, shifts in consumer behavior, etc., has proved quite difficult. This does not mean that deficits are not inflationary (they are), only that the quantitative evidence is inconclusive.

Another rationalization for deficits—one with more logic—is that federal deficits are not inflationary if the Fed does not print money to finance them. That might be true if the government seriously intended to pay off this year's deficit with next year's surplus. In that case, private savings would finance public spending, and the bonds issued to pay for this year's deficit would be retired by next year's surplus. At the end of

---

[3]A postwar high of 4 percent was set in FY 1976.

the period there would be no new Treasury obligations—cash or bonds —outstanding.

In practice it does not work that way. The government does not pay off its deficit next year or any year thereafter. Even if it prints no new cash to finance the deficit, it prints a torrent of other paper—bills, notes, and bonds. The nation's capital markets are very efficient in transforming those Treasury bills, notes, and bonds into cash at the discretion of the holder, so in practice they are "near money" and they can stimulate inflation. (The section on the financial causes of inflation elaborates on the inflationary impact of issuing Treasury securities.) The West German central bank is a good example of stubborn refusal to monetize its own government's deficit; but at best that policy only has limited inflation, not eliminated it.

When some public official asserts that deficits don't matter, an investor should remember the following: a federal deficit means that the government spends more than it receives. More spending means more aggregate demand in an economy already suffering from demand-induced inflation. Sooner or later (probably sooner), the extra demand created by federal deficits will find its outlet in inflation. Deficits do matter; they matter a great deal.

# THE SOCIAL CAUSES OF INFLATION

Excessive expectations and entitlements succinctly summarize the social causes of inflation.

The basic cause of inflation is too much demand for goods and services relative to the economy's ability to supply them. That excessive demand takes place on several levels: fiscal, financial, political, and social. The fiscal and financial causes of inflation are too many budget deficits and too many paper claims (e.g., money, bonds, etc.). The political cause is the oldest one in political history—using the public purse to buy votes. The social cause was expressed by the early labor leader Samuel Gompers. Confronted by an exasperated executive who demanded to know what the union wanted, Gompers replied, "More and more of more and more."

The desire for more generally remains latent when people have no realistic hope of getting it. In static economies before the industrial revolution, few people reasonably hoped that their standards of living would exceed those of their grandparents. For the generation which endured the depression of the 1930s and the war of the 1940s, disaster seemed the norm. Peace and growing prosperity seemed like unrealistically high expectations.

One of the most pleasant human events is to experience a reality far above expectations. The sustained economic growth of the 1950–1973 period was far above general expectations. The war in Vietnam was an unfortunate interruption to peace, but not to prosperity. From serious economists (who should have known better) to the general population, expectations about the future slowly improved from dismal to optimistic. Perpetually growing prosperity became not merely a hope but a general expectation.

The desire for more, always latent, burst forth. The economy could be expected to supply more regardless of how many burdens were placed on it to fight a foreign war, clean up the environment, provide more safety for workers, etc. The economy could be expected to supply more even though government was expanding its share of GNP and the work ethic was deteriorating. The economy could be expected to supply more even though economic incentives were reduced by high marginal tax rates for very productive individuals and by generous social welfare programs which made unemployment more attractive than work for many at the lower end of the economic spectrum. (Liberals justified those welfare programs out of compassion for the truly needy. Conservatives viewed them as producing perpetual parasites on the public purse.)

A psychologist might view the perpetual demand for more as an outpouring of infantile impulses. But those impulses make a major contribution to inflation. Consumers who expect more tomorrow become willing to borrow and spend today. Entrepreneurs who expect more consumer demand for their products tomorrow become willing to borrow and spend on new factories today. Politicians who respond to these expectations for more (in fairness, politicians do their bit to contribute to excessive expectations) spend more money, cut more taxes, and borrow more to do it. All that borrowing and spending creates the excessive demand which causes inflation.

Expecting more goods and services is one thing. Feeling entitled to them is something quite different. One of the remarkable features of the current inflation is how excessive expectations were transformed into entitlements, thereby making inflation worse and its cure far more painful.

An entitlement may be defined as an expectation plus a moral right that the expectation be fulfilled. One reasonably may expect the sun to rise in the east tomorrow morning without imposing any moral obligation on the sun to satisfy that expectation. When the subject shifts from the sun to goods and services, however, human beings are very willing to find reasons why they are morally entitled to have their expectations satisfied.

The people are rare who believe that they are not entitled to all that they receive. Those who work for a living generally feel entitled to at least the income they receive today and to more income tomorrow.[4] Most of those who do not work for a living also feel similarly entitled. Retirees feel entitled to their Social Security checks even if the actuarial value of their past payments to the system was far less than the benefits they now draw from it. Welfare mothers feel entitled to be supported by society regardless of their contribution to it. Those fortunate enough to possess earned or unearned wealth may have qualms about being entitled to the affluence they enjoy, but those qualms are seldom strong enough to prompt them to abandon their wealth and follow the biblical injunction of distributing their goods to the poor.

For reasons which appear very good to people who are persuaded by them, virtually all people feel morally entitled to at least their current level of goods and services, and probably more. When something happens to reduce people's level of real income (e.g., a recession) or to reduce their prospects of future increases in real income, their reaction is likely to be far stronger than the mere disappointment which accompanies an unfulfilled expectation. The reaction is likely to be outrage at being deprived of something to which they feel they are morally entitled.

Politicians are very sensitive to outraged constituents. Having encouraged the popular assumption that the government is responsible for managing the economy (an assumption not widely held until the last generation), politicians found themselves deluged by demands that the government do something whenever a recession began to threaten the voters' entitlements to more goods and services. The something that the government generally does in response to such voter outrage is to engage in massive fiscal and monetary stimulation to the economy, which leads to a brief pickup in the economy and to an inflationary hangover shortly thereafter.

Rising expectations and entitlements are the social cause of inflation. Reducing those expectations and entitlements is a necessary condition

---

[4]The General Motors–United Auto Workers contracts illustrated that feeling of entitlement by giving workers an annual raise of 3 percent plus a cost-of-living adjustment. That was little problem when those contracts began in the late 1940s, but the long-term result of such generosity was to make auto workers among the nation's highest paid industrial workers and to make GM's labor costs far higher than those abroad.

of ending it. Since reducing expectations produces disappointment and reducing entitlements engenders outrage, ending inflation is a fearful and painful process.

## FEAR AND PAIN

If inflation is viewed as a social disease, then its cure may be viewed as large doses of fear and pain, disagreeable as that prescription may sound. Fear and pain may be substituted for each other, but without a critical mass of both of them, inflation will accelerate.

Fear came quickly to the generation which endured the depression of the 1930s. Only a small amount of recessionary pain evoked expectations of a calamity to come. The recessions of the 1950s evoked enough fear in union leaders to make them more tractable about demanding higher wages; there was no sense in being too greedy when the security of jobs was at stake. Mild recessions also evoked great fear in business people who quickly became reasonable about raising prices, since they would lose market share to price-cutting competitors.

The price stability of the early 1960s owed much to the legacy of fear left over from the depression of the 1930s and to the recessions of the 1950s. Having been conditioned by catastrophe in the past, labor and business leaders simply did not *think* in terms of massive price increases. People generally fear the tiger which bit them last, and the last tiger to bite hard was depression.

There is a Burmese saying that the tiger which bites next is seldom the tiger which bit last. From the founding of this country until the 1940s, the U.S. economy spent over 40 percent of the time in recessions and depressions of varying severity and duration. From the 1950s on, however, the economy contracted less than 20 percent of the time. Even the few recessions which did take place were mild by comparison with the past. The new reality was that recession had become a toothless tiger.

| | Number of economic contractions | Number of months contracting | Percent of period contracting |
|---|---|---|---|
| 1938–1981 | 8 | 80 | 16 |
| 1895–1938 | 12 | 227 | 44 |
| 1854–1895 | 9 | 219 | 42 |

Perception lagged the new reality because old dogs seldom learn new tricks. Most people form their basic view of the world by their early twenties and go to their graves with that same view intact half a century later. Most of those who endured the depression of the 1930s as adults were not convinced that recession was no longer a reality; they simply died out by the early 1980s or had been put out to pasture and away from power.

The new generation which replaced the old one knew no fear. For them the depression was ancient history like the fall of Rome and the voyage of Columbus; it was not a reality likely to be repeated. The new generation grew up blessed with no personal memory of the pain of depression and no fear that they ever would have to face that pain.

The new generation had very different expectations as a result of its very different experiences. Recessions, on the rare occasions when they came, were expected to be brief. The federal government was expected to rush to the rescue with massive stimulus whenever recession raised its ugly head. Keynesian economists were expected to work their usual magic and to restore the economy to robust real growth. When the old generation saw a recession begin, they expected it would continue to widen into a chasm. When the new generation saw a recession widen from a ravine to valley, they confidently expected it to widen no more, and calmly looked across the valley to better times ahead. A generation ago a small amount of recessionary pain evoked a large amount of fear, but today even a large amount of recessionary pain evokes only a small amount of fear.

This radical change in expectations paralyzed the government's attempts to reduce inflation. Threats that terrible things would happen (former Fed chairman Arthur Burns was particularly good at sounding ominous) were not believed. Unemployment at levels once thought to be disastrous did not halt wage increases, because unemployment compensation mitigated the pain and the expectation of an imminent economic recovery eliminated the fear. (Unemployment at 6 percent, considered an awfully high level in the early 1970s, was considered a very desirable goal in the early 1980s when unemployment was double-digit.) Business people reasoned in a similar fashion, since prospective federal bailouts mitigated the pain of bankruptcy, so prices were as unresponsive to recession as wages.

Creating a risk-free society has major advantages from a humanitarian perspective, but disastrous consequences from an economic one. Without either fear or pain to restrain them, business people are free to raise wages and prices in a never-ending spiral. Inflation is not merely a set of numbers about deficits and money supply, but a way of thinking and acting by millions of participants in the economy. Without either fear or pain, government has no lever to change the inflationary ways its people think and act.

## THE STICKY ECONOMY

Most wages and prices are sticky on the downside, a condition which creates a cruel dilemma for anti-inflationary policy.

In theory, full employment can be maintained in an economy with mild deflation if wages, prices, rents, and interest rates are fully adjustable downward. In practice, workers, business people, landlords, and lenders fight hard to prevent cuts in their nominal incomes. Even in the 1930s, workers and business leaders resisted declines in their nominal wages and prices. Today they fight much harder because they have much less fear of the consequences in the form of unemployment and lost market share. Once cut, wages and prices are hard to restore to their former levels; so keeping them up in spite of temporarily weak demand seems like a sensible course of action.

Sticky wages and prices make anti-inflationary policy very painful. Policies such as tax increases and tight money which are intended to push down on inflation actually push down on real output instead. Confronted by weak demand, business people cut production rather than prices. Confronted by layoffs, unions hang tough in wage negotiations until unemployment soars far into double digits (e.g., the United Auto Workers).

Stickiness, unfortunately, is only on the downside. The first response to weak demand is to cut output rather than prices, but the first response to strong demand is to raise prices rather than output. This lack of symmetry places an anti-inflationary policy in a no-win situation. There is no painless way to cut inflation a little without cutting output a lot, and there is no pleasurable way to stimulate output a little without stimulating inflation a lot.

Like most generalizations, the stickiness of wages and prices has its exceptions. Nonunionized labor without the power to strike tends to be less sticky than organized labor in its approach to wage demands. Fighting for wage increases and against wage decreases is the major justification for a union leader's existence. Commodities such as copper and lumber which are sold in competitive markets are far less sticky than products such as autos and steel which are sold under conditions of limited competition. If the economy had more goods and services sold under very competitive conditions, their sticky wages and prices would not be such a barrier to effective anti-inflation policy.

# THE INVISIBLE HAND POINTS
# THE WRONG WAY

One of the earliest and best concepts in economics is that of the *invisible hand* which guides self-interested individuals in directions beneficial to society as a whole. Farmers may care only about the money they will receive for their crops, but the urban population which consumes them still benefits. Carpenters who diligently work to earn money for their families still benefit the people who enjoy shelters as a result of their efforts. Self-interest is the dynamic force which motivates people, and the invisible hand channels their efforts in directions which are good for the whole economy. In the same year that Adam Smith wrote about the invisible hand in economics, Benjamin Franklin expressed the same concept in politics to some reluctant signers of the Declaration of Independence: "We must all hang together, or assuredly we shall all hang separately."

What Smith did not realize, however, is that the invisible hand points the right way only in a positive sum economy with stable prices and real growth. In a zero sum inflationary economy, the invisible hand points self-interested individuals in directions which are irrelevant or destructive to the long-run welfare of the economy as a whole.

In an inflationary economy, the Puritan virtues of hard work, frugal saving, and productive investment became obsolete. Why work hard when the path to wealth lies through speculating on assets likely to benefit from inflation? Investors who bought gold at the start of the 1970s enjoyed a 2000 percent increase in price without doing a bit of work. Why save money when there is a negative real return on saving? Borrowing at a negative real rate of interest to buy assets such as apartments likely to go up in value is a far better way to get rich than is frugal saving. Why invest in productive new assets when the return on existing assets is higher? When the stock market began to value corporate assets at a discount from their replacement value in the early 1970s, investing in new plant and equipment became the *least* profitable investment for the average company (more on this in the next chapter).

The invisible hand works well when individuals believe that the path to their own future personal wealth lies through the Puritan values of hard work, frugal saving, and productive investment. The tragedy of inflation is that those values become obsolete. The new values which replace the old Puritan ones might be summarized as clever speculation with borrowed money. A whole generation has grown up with the attitude that getting ahead in life consists of clever speculation rather than the productive effort which benefits the rest of society.

As the Puritan values die, so does the moral legitimacy of income and wealth. In a period of stable prices, those who grow rich generally do so by working harder, saving more, and investing better than their peers. There is a large claim to moral legitimacy for their income and wealth when they earned them in that fashion. There is little claim to moral legitimacy, however, when income and wealth are obtained by clever speculation which benefits no one but the holder. Buying assets likely to appreciate in price is the way for an individual to get rich in an inflationary economy, but the legitimacy of those riches is destroyed by the method used to obtain them.

## SECULAR INFLATION

Since speculators obtain their ill-deserved riches from a rising secular inflation, that concept requires a bit of explanation.

The concept is easier than its precise measurement. *Secular inflation* is the level of price increase built into the economy on a long-term basis. Secular inflation is the broad trend of prices after allowing for monthly, seasonal, annual, and cyclical variations around the long-term trend.

The rate of secular inflation was near zero in the early 1960s when the Keynesians' "new economics" first began to stimulate the economy. By the late 1970s it had risen to 10 percent. The rise from 0 percent to 10 percent was not straight, but rather a crooked path which showed wide variations around a generally rising trend. The major cause of those variations was the business cycle; inflation generally peaks just after a business cycle top and bottoms about a year after a recession ends. Within each business cycle there were periods of unusual fluctuation due to crop shortgages, oil embargoes, etc.

Secular inflation is the rate embedded into wages, prices, and interest rates. If labor expects inflation to average 10 percent over the next 3 years, then it will demand wages of that amount and a little extra to reflect productivity gains. If investors expect 10 percent inflation, then they will demand, say, 13 percent to compensate for inflation and give them a small real rate of return. If business managers expect their wages and interest costs to go up by over 10 percent next year, then they will increase their prices at least 10 percent to compensate for those increased costs and to provide a boost to profits.

The concept of secular inflation allows the investor to focus on the long-run trend rather than on the short-run fluctuations. Translating that concept into a specific number is difficult, but a good approximation is the average of two numbers:

*The rate of change in wage costs over the last year less 1 percent for productivity gains.* Wages account for two-thirds of the GNP deflator and tend to be less volatile than many other measures of inflation. While productivity gains show a large amount of volatility over short periods, their long-term rate of improvement now appears to be 1 to 2 percent.

*The rate of change in the consumer price index (CPI) over the last 12 months.* The CPI is affected by factors such as crop shortages and oil embargoes over short periods, but when combined with labor costs it gives a fair approximation of secular inflation

## KEYNES IN ECLIPSE

The tragic fate of a good new idea is to reach its zenith of popularity coincident with its nadir of utility. The idea of a self-correcting laissez-faire economy was very popular in 1929, just as the economy itself went into a self-destructing downward spiral.

It took Keynes to show the next generation of economists how to use fiscal stimulus to correct the economy's depressionary defect. By the time Richard Nixon declared himself to be a Keynesian in 1971, however, Keynes's ideas were finished as the solution to the economy's relevant problems. Worse yet, Keynes's overzealous followers became a menace to the economy and the cause of the major problem of the 1970s—inflation.

The economy may be viewed like a car. When Keynes wrote his *General Theory* in 1936,[5] the major economies of the world were stuck in reverse or neutral and no one knew how to get them moving again. Keynes's contribution to economics was to point out the fiscal accelerator of deficit spending as a way to get the economy moving forward.

A little pressure on the fiscal accelerator was the perfect solution to get the economy moving forward. If the Keynesians had the sense to stop at a little pressure, then this chapter on the zero sum economy would not be necessary. Since the Keynesians were persons of abundant zeal and insufficient intellect, however, they did not stop with a little pressure on the fiscal accelerator, but instead pushed it to the floor. Too much pressure on the fiscal accelerator sent the economy careering out of control and into an inflationary boom. Only when inflation was far

[5]John M. Keynes, *General Theory of Employment, Interest, and Money,* Harcourt Brace Jovanovich (Harbinger), New York, 1964.

out of control did the Keynesians realize that Keynes's ideas were asymmetrical—they pointed to the accelerator but not to the brake.

First-rate thinkers often are cursed with second-rate followers, and Keynes was no exception. Like the sorcerer's apprentice, Keynes's followers knew how to start the flow of fiscal stimulus but not how to stop it. Worse still, they were reluctant to admit that fiscal stimulus had gone from the solution to one problem (i.e., depression) to the cause of another (i.e., inflation). Admitting that excessive fiscal stimulus was part of the problem rather than part of the solution was tantamount to admitting that they were obsolete, because stimulating the economy was the only thing most Keynesians knew how to do. The Keynesians spent their professional lives developing ever more refined answers to the question of what to do about depression, but, much to their discomfort, that was no longer the relevant question in the 1960s and 1970s. The relevant question was what to do about the inflation that the zealous Keynesians had caused by their excessive fiscal stimulus.

It was a tragic irony for those who had begun their professional careers as zealous young rebels, rising up against the confused and obsolete economics establishment of the 1930s. By the mid 1960s the hot young rebels had become the new economics establishment, sure of themselves and basking in the glory that came with slaying the dragon of depression. When the dragon of inflation reared its head, the Keynesians found themselves in the awkward position of French generals: admirably prepared for the last war and totally perplexed by the present one. By the mid 1970s the Keynesians had gone full circle to become the confused and obsolete economics establishment against which other zealous young rebels were rising up.

When Karl Marx was old and gray, he looked at his zealous, confused followers and said, "I am not a Marxist," a statement which has bewildered fervent Marxists ever since. If Keynes had lived long enough to see the havoc caused by his own zealous, confused followers, he might have declared himself not to be a Keynesian. No one knows for sure. Keynes was well aware of the dangers of inflation, but in the 1930s that was not a relevant problem. If he had any idea of the extreme to which his fervent followers would have taken his ideas about fiscal stimulus, he might have given them the same advice Talleyrand gave to his young diplomats: "not too much zeal."

While inflation was not the relevant problem during Keynes's lifetime, he was well aware of its dangers, as shown by the following short essay:

Lenin is said to have declared that the best way to destroy the capitalist system was to debauch the currency. By a continuing process of inflation, governments can confiscate, secretly and unobserved, an important part of the wealth of their citizens. By this method they not only confiscate, but they confiscate arbitrarily; and while the process impoverishes many, it actually enriches some.

The sight of this arbitrary rearrangement of riches strikes not only at security, but at confidence in the equity of the existing distribution of wealth. Those to whom the system brings windfalls, beyond their deserts and even beyond their expectations or desires, become [obscene] "profiteers," who are the object of the hatred of the [middle class] whom the inflation has impoverished, not less than the [working people].

As the inflation proceeds and the real value of the currency fluctuates wildly from month to month, all permanent relations between debtors and creditors, which form the ultimate foundation of capitalism, become so utterly disordered as to be almost meaningless; and the process of wealth-getting degenerates into a gamble.

Lenin was certainly right. There is no subtler, no surer means of overturning the existing basis of society than to debauch the currency. The process engages all the hidden forces of economic law on the side of destruction, and does it in a manner which not one man in a million is able to diagnose. . . .

Governments, being many of them at this moment reckless in their methods as well as weak, seek to direct on to a class known as "profiteers" the popular indignation against the more obvious consequences of their [own] vicious methods. These "profiteers" are, broadly speaking, the entrepreneur class of capitalists, that is to say, the active and constructive element in the whole capitalist society, who in a period of rapidly rising prices cannot but get rich quick whether they wish it or desire it or not. If prices are continually rising, every trader who has purchased for [inventory] or owns property and plant inevitably makes profits.

By directing hatred against this class, therefore, the governments are carrying a step further the fatal process which the subtle mind of Lenin had consciously conceived. The profiteers are a consequence of Lenin and not a cause of rising prices. By combining a popular hatred of the class of entrepreneurs with the blow already given to social security by the violent and arbitrary disturbance of contract and of the established equilibrium of wealth which is the inevitable result of inflation, these governments are fast rendering impossible a continuance of the social and economic order. . . . But they have no plan for replacing it.[6]

---

[6]Keynes, *The Collected Writings of John Maynard Keynes*, vol. 2: *The Economic Consequences of Peace*, Macmillan, New York, 1971, pp. 148-149.

# THE PHILIPS CURVE

The rise and fall of the Philips curve neatly traced the rise and fall of Keynesian economics. While not formally a part of Keynes's theory (the idea came from another British economist two decades after Keynes wrote his *General Theory*), the Philips curve quickly became a major article of faith in neo-Keynesian dogma. Today it lies in richly deserved disrepute.

In its original form, the Philips curve suggested that there is a stable trade-off between inflation and real growth. Countries with stable prices seemed to have low-growth economies, while countries with high-growth rates of real growth had somewhat higher rates of inflation. (High inflation at the time was still in single digits except in banana republics.) Leaping from objective observation of past facts to hopeful prediction of future ones, Keynesians asserted that by accepting a little more inflation for a little more growth, society would benefit.

Accepting a little more inflation to achieve a lot more real growth seemed like a good idea at the time, but a little inflation is no more harmless than a little pregnancy. As time went by, a little more inflation became a lot more. As soon as the government became willing to accept 2 percent inflation, it got 4 percent. When it became willing to accept 4 percent, it got 6 to 8 percent. Only in the 1970s did the government economists begin to realize that the trade-off between inflation and real growth was an *accelerating* one, not a stable one. The only way to maintain a high level of real growth was to accept an ever-increasing level of inflation. When the inflation rate rose to levels intolerable at the time, measures to control inflation (e.g., tight money and tax hikes) were introduced which turned high real growth into serious recession.

To the extent that it worked at all, the Philips curve did so by fooling people about the real level of inflation. If most people thought that inflation was running at 2 percent, then the government could achieve a temporary stimulus to real growth by loose fiscal and monetary policies which would produce inflation of 4 percent in the end. Business leaders who felt the stimulus at first responded with a higher output of goods and services until they ran into limits to physical capacity and labor availability. At that point they raised prices, labor raised wages, and inflation accelerated to well beyond its previous levels.

With each passing business cycle, fewer and fewer people were fooled by the trick the government played on them. Each time the government stimulated the economy, more people learned to respond with higher wages and prices rather than with higher real output. When the government first began to stimulate the economy deliberately in the early 1960s, $1 of stimulus might produce as much as $0.80

of real growth and $0.20 of inflation. Twenty years later the same $1 of stimulus was generating no more than $0.20 of real growth and $0.80 of inflation. Like an addict who must use increasing amounts of a drug to achieve the same pleasant effect, the government had to inject increasing amounts of stimulus into the economy to achieve the same effect in real terms.

In the long run there is no Philips curve. By stimulating the economy beyond its noninflationary potential, the Keynesians generated more growth on a temporary basis. The price of curing that inflation is a stagnant, recessionary economy (see Chapter 2). When the period of above-average growth is averaged with the following period of below-average growth (1973 to ?), it is unlikely that anything will have been gained.

# FOR BETTER OR WORSE, BUT NOT THE SAME

When the Philips curve died, so did the seductive notion that there is any stable rate of inflation above zero. Like virginity, stable prices are capable of maintenance rather than restoration.

The notion that there was some positive but stable rate of inflation rested on the assumption that inflation would stop when unemployment rose. When both unemployment and inflation rose together in the 1970s, an event the Keynesians once believed impossible, they fell back to the position that there was some particular level of unemployment (e.g., 6 percent then 8 percent) which would bring price stability. When that did not happen either, they did not know what to think or do.

People will expend great intellectual energy to avoid facing an unpleasant fact, and the expenditure of energy generally correlates well with the unpleasantness of the fact they are trying to avoid. The most unpleasant fact that Keynesians tried to avoid about inflation was its instability above zero. In economic terms, any positive inflation rate is an unstable equilibrium with a bimodal distribution (a two-humped curve like a camel's back, rather than the more common single hump of a normal distribution) of probabilities as to its further rate. In plain English, inflation will get much better or much worse, but it will not stay the same.

The absence of any stable inflation above zero also meant the absence of any acceptable economic policy. Reducing deeply embedded inflation meant accepting a deeply painful depression which Keynesians had devoted their lives to curing and preventing. Accepting ever-escalating inflation was equally unacceptable. The absence of a practical middle ground in dealing with inflation meant that Keynesians were impaled on the horns of a dilemma of their own making.

## NONSOLUTIONS TO INFLATION

The effective cures to inflation are painful, and the painless cures are ineffective. That unpleasant correlation between pain and effectiveness is the most important and most frantically ignored fact in dealing with inflation.

The least effective and most popular solution to inflation is to blame someone else. Management blames greedy labor and bloated government. Labor blames greedy management. Everyone blames the Arabs in OPEC. Blaming is an effective way to discharge self-righteous indignation, but it is a totally ineffective way to cure inflation.

Incomes policy (also called *wage and price controls*) is King Canute's way of dealing with inflation. The good king believed that he could command the tide not to rise, a belief which lasted until he got his feet wet. Passing laws which forbid wages and prices to rise does not stem the rise permanently. At best an incomes policy diverts and delays the surge in prices. Used in conjunction with monetary and fiscal restraint, an incomes policy could be effective. Its more common use, however, is as a substitute for unpopular monetary and fiscal restraint.

Monetary restraint is a more effective cure for inflation, and a more painful one. As long as a country is not starting from a position of intolerable inflation or recession, limiting the growth of the money supply to 2 to 3 percent per year is a good prescription for avoiding both. When a country starts from a position of intolerable inflation, several problems arise.

> The demand for money and credit generally exceeds supply, leading to competition among borrowers. The federal government's borrowing always wins out, followed closely by large corporations. The losers in the competition are weaker borrowers who are "crowded out," such as those borrowing for home building and autos.

> The rate of interest is the price of money. If price is used to ration a scarce amount of money, then interest rates soar to very high levels in real terms. After years of becoming accustomed to low or negative rates of interest, beleaguered borrowers may face the twin pains of an inadequate supply of money and a very high price for the little they obtain.

Choosing which definition of the money supply to control is more than an academic exercise in a world where financial innovation is changing the nature of money. Whatever definition of money the Fed selects to control is likely to become the least relevant as creative bankers and financiers develop new ways to circumvent it. NOW accounts are a creative way to destroy the legal distinction between savings accounts and liquid checking accounts. Money market mutual funds are an innovation to circumvent the Fed's limits on the amount of interest a bank can pay by taking money from low-interest bank accounts and transforming it into high-interest certificates of deposit. The entire Eurodollar market may be viewed as a vehicle created by bankers to use in escaping the restrictions imposed by their own central banks.

Closely related to the problem of defining money supply in a world of financial innovation is how to control the other elements of the paper economy. Bonds, commercial paper, and credit instruments are "near money" which may substitute in practice for the definition of the money supply which the Fed is actively trying to control. Even if credit can be controlled, there is still the issue of how to stop the cancerous growth of entitlements in the form of government-guaranteed entitlements such as pension rights and welfare payments.

Monetary policy is a long-term tool in a short-term world. The costs of unemployment, lost output, and bankruptcies are painfully apparent in the short run, while the benefits of stable prices may be painfully long in coming. Applying monetary restraint effectively means being willing to ignore the inevitable pressures which come with rising unemployment and declining profits in a recession. The usual pattern of central bankers is to act tough until a growing recession generates enough political pressure to induce them to make a U turn by stimulating the money supply. Monetary policy is an effective tool which few nations have the will to use for a long enough period to produce lasting results.

Monetary policy alone, like incomes policy alone, is not enough to do the job. Fiscal policy also must be restrained so that the federal budget is at least near balance and preferably in surplus. Currently most western governments are running huge budget deficits while maintaining tight monetary policies. Not surprisingly, that combination of policies does not work well. Pressing firmly on both the fiscal accelerator and the monetary brake generates the same results for both an economy and for a car: it doesn't go far, but the friction of conflicting forces slowly tears it apart.

Like monetary policy, supply-side policies have some appeal as the solution to inflation. Since no one likes the painful process of lowering aggregate demand, then why not raise supply? While many supply-side policies (e.g., reducing excessive regulation, lowering marginal tax rates) have merit, they are not *the* solution to inflation:

> Even if supply-side policies were extremely successful, they would not do the job completely. Raising the secular growth of productivity by 2 percent per year would be a real (and, unfortunately, unlikely) triumph for supply-side economics, but that achievement would offset only a part of the secular inflation rate, which is far higher than 2 percent.

> Supply-side economics assumes that business people will be encouraged to invest heavily, but currently they are doing the opposite. There is no point in building new capacity when their existing capacity is operating at a fraction of its total potential.

> The mix of fiscal and monetary policies suggested by supply has inherent contradictions. If taxes are cut to stimulate the economy, then the federal deficit will widen. If the Fed maintains a tight money policy, then that wide federal deficit will preempt a large share of the nation's personal savings which otherwise would have gone into private sector investment. If the Fed is accommodative enough to finance both the wide federal deficit and private investment, then it is likely to touch off a new round of inflation.

> Like monetary policy, supply-side economics shows beneficial results largely in the long run. Its overzealous advocates oversold it during the early days of the Reagan administration in terms of both how large the benefits would be and how soon they would be realized. The inevitable short-term disillusion which set in generated a bias against further supply-side measures, some of which had considerable long-term merit.

Like supply-side economics, the "rational-expectations" school of economics offers a partial solution to inflation. Its proponents correctly note that attitudes and expectations play a major role in setting wages and prices, and then they proceed to a dubious policy recommendation.

If the government clearly announces to the world its intention to adopt noninflationary fiscal and monetary policies, they reason, then people will adjust their expectations and behavior accordingly. The obvious problem with that view is that no sane person really believes the government is sincere about ending inflation for good. After years of talking tough and then resorting to massive fiscal and monetary stimulus as soon as unemployment begins to rise, government officials have a credibility so low that few people would believe them even if they really were determined to end inflation for good. The obituary for the rational-expectations solution to inflation might read, "Ambushed at Credibility Gap."

The nonsolutions and partial solutions to inflation are very popular for understandable reasons. No one likes the idea of a depression, so everyone searches for a less painful alternative. The fact which no one wants to face, however, is that there is no painless alternative to recession as a means to change the inflationary behavior of labor, business, government, and the nation's capital markets. History offers no encouraging examples of a deeply embedded inflation which ended painlessly. The current inflation, like others in the past, will not have a soft landing.

# RECOGNIZING THE ZERO SUM ECONOMY

The following indicators are useful in recognizing an inflationary economy:

1. *The monetary policy.* If real interest rates are flat or negative, then the economy is likely to have an inflationary bias. If the *broadly* defined measures of the money supply expand more rapidly than real GNP, then excess purchasing power is being created which probably will find its outlet in rising prices. Inflation is not just a monetary phenomenon, but the forces which create it always find their expression in excessive monetary growth and low or negative real interest rates.

2. *Fiscal policy.* There are some situations where a federal deficit is desirable, but perpetual deficits lead to excessive growth of aggregate demand in the economy. If conventional wisdom comes to regard federal deficits as virtuous, then there is little hope of a balanced, noninflationary budget. Ideally the measure of a balanced budget should include off-budget items and the present value of unfunded pensions and social security entitlements, but in practice they are difficult to calculate, and the stated budget deficit will do very well.

3. *The social-political indication.* If most people feel entitled to an ever-increasing standard of living, demand is likely. If price stability is taken for granted (as in the early 1960s) or if it is considered a low priority (e.g., low unemployment may be more important), then it is unlikely to be maintained. Once set in motion, inflation requires a powerful social and political consensus to bear the pain necessary to end it.

4. *Momentum.* Perhaps the easiest way to anticipate future inflation is to look at the past. If inflation has been present on average over the last 4 years (i.e., the length of a president's term in office), then it is likely to be present over the next 4 years too. Inflation develops such a powerful momentum that an investor may assume that it will continue unless a powerful depression stops it.

# CHAPTER FIVE

# THE ZERO SUM INVESTING GAME

The zero sum investing game was easy to play when inflation accelerated in the 1970s. Inflation hedges were cheap, and lenders were naive enough to lend money at single-digit rates in an economy experiencing double-digit price increases. Neither of those two conditions prevails today. Inflation hedges are not very cheap, and badly burned lenders are lending money at double-digit rates in an economy experiencing single-digit price increases. The zero sum investing game will be far more difficult to play in the 1980s than in the 1970s, but an investor will have no other choice as long as the economy's inflation rate exceeds its growth rate.

## THE FEDERAL RESERVE CHANGES THE RULES OF THE GAME

Rarely does a single change in government policy produce a sweeping, long-term change in the rules of the game for investors. One of those rare changes took place in the fall of 1979 when the Federal Reserve switched from controlling interest rates to controlling the money supply.

Like any other commodity, money has both a quantity and a price (i.e., interest is the price of money). Also like any other commodity, controlling the price of money at an artificially low level stimulates an excessive demand for it. Until October 1979, the Fed's official policy was to control short-term interest rates. Its unofficial but no less implemented policy was to use its control powers to keep interest rates at low levels to satisfy political demands for cheap money. Keeping interest rates at or below the level of inflation created a bargain for borrowers, but all that borrowing and spending resulted in excessive money supply growth and its usual result—inflation. After years of tinkering with its procedures to control interest rates without success, the Fed reluctantly accepted the necessity of a major change to become more effective in combating inflation.

Like St. Paul on the road to Damascus, the Fed experienced a dramatic conversion in October 1979. After generations of controlling interest rates, the Fed changed to a new policy of controlling the money supply. The monetarists at first rejoiced that the Fed had seen the light and embraced their economic faith. Later the more devout monetarists accused the Fed of heresy because the money supply grew in an irregular fashion. Whatever its degree of conversion to monetarism, the Fed created major changes in the level and the volatility of interest rates.

Interest rates went up; they went up to new records in nominal terms at both the long and the short ends of the yield curve. They went up in inflation-adjusted terms too, thereby creating a revolution in the relationship between borrower and lender. A major shift in the nation's financial balance of power took place as interest rates rose from below the secular rate of inflation to well above, and inflation hedges have not been the same since.

As interest rates went up, they became more volatile. In the first 2 years following the Fed's new policy, the average price change in long-term government bonds was three times its average of the previous decade. Other interest rates underwent similar convulsive changes. For investors accustomed to low and stable interest rates, the high and volatile ones which followed the Fed's new policy were more than just a shock; they significantly increased the dangers and reduced the opportunities to capitalize on inflation.

Just how long the Fed will hold to its new policy is the obvious question in light of the Fed's poor record in the past. The Fed's past policy was to declare war on inflation, adopt a restrictive monetary stance, and promise to persevere until prices became stable. As soon as tight money produced a recession and rising unemployment, however, promises were forgotten and the war against inflation was abandoned. To fight recession, the Fed lowered interest rates and increased the money supply, which not surprisingly led to an increase in inflation some time later. Then the whole cycle started over again, but with two significant differences. The interval between an increase in the money supply and an increase in inflation became shorter with each passing cycle as more people came to understand the Fed's game. The second difference was that increasingly massive amounts of money supply growth were necessary to achieve the same stimulative effect on real economic growth, a situation similar to an addict whose rising tolerance to a drug requires ever more massive doses to achieve the same effect.

The gap between the Fed's promises and its performance suggests scepticism about how long it will pursue its new policy of controlling money supply growth. Scepticism, however, should not be confused with total disbelief. There is always a chance that the Fed will stay the course and surprise everyone, including itself. Even if the Fed eventually caves in, it may pursue its new policy long enough to devastate a good many investors, as anyone who held gold or real estate in the 1979–1982 period knows only too well. There is also a question of whether the Fed can go back to its old policy now that the genie of high and volatile interest rates is out of the bottle. The recent structural changes in the nation's financial markets (e.g., more competition among providers of financial services, deregulation of interest rates) also make it more difficult for the Fed to return to its old inflationary way. Even when the Fed switched to a stimulative policy in the fall of 1982, interest rates remained at sharply positive levels in real terms.

# NO PLACE TO HIDE

Conventional wisdom says that assets such as gold and real estate are marvelous inflation hedges. Conventional wisdom is only partly right. Gold and real estate enjoyed excellent real returns in the 1970s with only an occasional correction. That does not mean , however, that they will be the premier inflation hedges in the 1980s. The unpleasant fact is that there is no perfect and permanent hedge against inflation.

*Inflation hedge* is simply another term for a stable store of value. Money traditionally filled that role, so that its real value stayed roughly the same over long periods of time. As best as economists have been able to reconstruct it, the wholesale price index in Britain was at the same level in 1910 that it was in 1610. Except for a few brief fluctuations during the interim, money did an admirable job of providing a long-term store of value. The principal reason for this extended period of remarkable price stability was the gold standard which prevented politicians from debasing the currency.

Inflation means that money no longer fills its traditional role as a store of value. People may differ as to how much inflation they think our economy will experience over the next decade, but almost everyone believes that a dollar then will buy less than a dollar today. Inflation before World War II generally ended in a swift depression, so faith in the value of money was left intact. The crucial difference this time is that inflation has gone on so long that most people regard the depreciating dollar as normal. The popular belief that the dollar will certainly depreciate by some uncertain amount in real terms means that the dollar has abdicated its role as a store of value.

Nothing has arisen to take the dollar's place. There is no asset an investor can look to which will provide complete protection against inflation with reasonable safety. Even the best assets are likely to provide only partial protection some of the time.

The volatility which inflation creates is the reason there is no perfect hedge against it. As inflation increases, so does the volatility of asset prices. The Fed's new operating policy contributes to volatile interest rates, but the reason for volatility runs much deeper. Investors are searching for a stable store of value, and their search becomes increasingly desperate as inflation rises. They become more and more frantic in their futile search for a stable store of value and rush from one asset to another in hopes of finding something—anything—which will keep up with inflation. Their rush causes them to dump one asset to buy another, creating ever more volatile prices of the assets they are buying and selling.

The chapters on the positive and negative sum investing games divide assets into winners and losers. No such easy division of assets is possible in this chapter because there is no perfect and permanent hedge against inflation. Instead each asset's merits are examined to show when it is likely to outperform inflation and when it is likely to produce losses for its investors.

# BONDS

For over 30 years, bonds drove investors down the road of genteel poverty. Inflation destroyed the real value of principal and interest payments. As interest rates rose along with inflation, the nominal-value bonds declined as well.

In a generation accustomed to double-digit rates for both interest and inflation, it seems incredible that the U.S. Treasury and AT&T once sold long-term bonds at interest rates of 3 percent or less. In 1981 triple-A telephone yields rose above 17 percent, reducing the market value of those older bonds to a fraction of their original value. Inflation took over where interest rates left off by reducing the real value of the bonds even more.

Investment theory suggests that bond yields consist of two elements: a real rate (generally assumed to be 3 percent, but which in fact may be less) and an inflation premium. Investment practice suggests that the inflation premium never quite catches up to the accelerating rate of inflation. Throughout most of the 1970s, the coupons on new bonds went up, the prices of old bonds went down, and bond investors suffered financial euthanasia. The moral seemed very clear: Avoid all bonds!

Today the situation is far less clear. Bond yields consist of not just two elements but three: a real rate, an inflation premium, and a fear component. The relevant fear is that inflation will accelerate to new heights when the Fed caves in again and abandons the fight against inflation just as it has in the past. As this book is written, the three elements of yield on 12 percent AAA telephone bonds are approximately as follows:

Inflation premium—5 percent
Real rate of interest—2 to 3 percent
Fear premium—4 to 5 percent

The existence of a large fear component means that *investors are being paid to take the risk of owning bonds* for the first time in a generation. For today's 12 percent bond to provide negative real returns, inflation must return to double digits. There was a time when double-digit inflation was a quaint Latin American malady, not a disease likely to strike North America. The experience of the 1970s demonstrates that the risk of high inflation is a very real one, but the difference today lies in popular expectations. Few people in the 1970s expected double-digit inflation, so interest rates were too low to compensate bondholders for that risk. Today many people expect renewed inflation, particularly those bondholders who were so badly burned over the last generation. The lingering memories of how inflation ravaged the real returns in bonds are the reason that bondholders are so cautious and that the fear premium in bonds is so high. There is no such thing as a riskless investment; only an investment with risks the investor is being well-paid to take. The large fear component in bond yields today is an investor's incentive to take the risk of owning bonds, but there is never any guarantee that the feared resurgence of inflation will not come to pass.

Bonds are no longer for widows and orphans, a fact painfully apparent to the impoverished widows and orphans who have owned them during the past 30 years. For investors who can assume the risk, the scenarios under which to buy and sell bonds are:

Buy bonds *after* the Fed tightens monetary policy to fight inflation, after the clash of private and public demands for credit have driven interest rates at least 5 percent above the secular rate of inflation, and *after* the economy clearly has begun to contract. Those three rules cannot guarantee that the investor will buy at the absolute bottom (no set of rules can guarantee that), but they will keep investors out of bonds during periods of maximum risk and keep them in bonds when they have a good chance of receiving both a real current rate of return and a capital gain.

Sell or avoid bonds when the opposite conditions prevail: *after* (preferably soon after) the Fed loosens monetary policy to stimulate the economy out of recession, after the nominal interest rate on bonds drops to less than 5 percent above the secular inflation rate, and *after* a business cycle recovery is clearly under way.

So far the emphasis has been on federal and high-quality bonds which offer both quality and liquidity. For the investor who can afford the *additional* risk of lower-quality bonds, the following comments may be helpful.

Outright defaults have been rare, and bondholders generally are well-paid to take the additional risk of a rare default in low-quality bonds. Payment for taking the risk of default comes in the form of quality spreads, or the difference between the yield on high-quality bonds and the yield on low-quality ones. Yield spreads in the postwar period have been excessive relative to the small risk of default, which is another way of saying that investors in low-quality bonds have done much better than investors in high-quality ones.

The low risk of default in the past generation does not equate to a similar low risk in the 1980s. Inflation often ends in a bang, and when that bang comes, the defaults on low-quality bonds may rise sharply (see Chapter 2).

Defaults come in waves, not as a steady stream. Defaults rarely occur when the economy is expanding vigorously and business conditions are robust. Almost anyone can make money then. Defaults generally bunch up toward the tail end of a major recession such as the one which took place in 1973 to 1975. Several years may go by with no significant defaults at all, then a group of them will hit all at once during a depression.

The best time to buy low-quality bonds is after fear of deepening recession has caused quality spreads to widen. The quality spread between AAA bonds and Baa bonds widened from 100 basis points in early 1980 to 270 basis points in the fall of 1982 as the economy contracted. An incredible 600 basis points separated AAA bonds from Baa ones during the depths of the depression in 1932. *Moody's Bond Record,* available at the business section of most large libraries, contains abundant information on yield spreads for the serious bond investor.

Selection is the key problem. Very few casual investors have the time, expertise, and access to information necessary to separate the wheat from the chaff. Professional investors do have the time, expertise, and knowledge to perform the selection job well, so they often have a decisive advantage over their casual counterparts.

Professional investors also have an advantage in negotiating commissions, which can be much larger for low-quality bonds than for high-quality ones. After all, the objective for investors is to enrich themselves, not their brokers.

The normal rating services such as Moody's and Standard and Poor's are good guides to bond quality, but not perfect ones. Their rating changes often take place *after* a company's fortunes have changed for better or worse, not before. In general, the investor is better off avoiding sunset industries such as steel and autos which need constant infusions of new cash merely to survive; their bond ratings have been declining for years and are likely to continue in that direction. The risk of default is likely to be less in sunrise industries such as telecommunication which may need outside financing to grow and thrive, but whose long-term future is now promising in the best case and whose assets are likely to be more marketable in the worst case.

Investors who want to learn more about the mechanics of bond yields may read *Inside the Yield Book* by Martin Liebowitz and Sidney Homer.[1]

---

[1]Published by Prentice-Hall, Englewood Cliffs, N.J., 1973.

## CASH EQUIVALENTS

Holding cash in an inflationary world is a guarantee of loss in real terms. A better policy is to hold cash equivalents in the form of riskless obligations of the federal government, riskless deposits insured by the federal government at banks and savings and loan associations, and low-risk deposits in money market mutual funds. A few money market funds hold only assets issued or insured by the federal government, so they also may be considered riskless instead of merely low-risk.

In the 30 years before the Fed implemented its new policy in 1979, an investment strategy of rolling over Treasury bills would have yielded returns roughly the same as the inflation rate. Just keeping up with inflation does not sound very glamorous, but it was a much better strategy than buying bonds.

Since the Fed began its new policy in October 1979, the returns on cash. equivalents have been 2 to 7 percent higher than inflation. They are likely to stay that way as long as the Fed sticks to its guns. In both Europe and the United States, large government deficits cause upward pressure on demand (and hence on demand-induced inflation) which central banks offset by tight monetary policies. The result of this collision between fiscal and monetary policies is high interest rates, which clearly benefit holders of short-term cash equivalents. The return on cash equivalents is almost certain to be volatile in addition to being positive in real terms, but then volatility is a fact of life which investors must learn to live with.

There are two risks in holding cash equivalents. If the Fed reverts to its old policy of stimulating growth in the money supply to fight recession and unemployment, then the real return on cash equivalents may slip into negative territory. Even at worst, however, negative real returns on cash equivalents are likely to be brief and moderate. More serious is the risk of opportunity loss. There will be many opportunities to achieve sharply positive real returns for investors willing to take the additional risk of other assets such as stocks, bonds, real estate, and gold.

Willing or not, taxable investors have no choice but to take that additional risk if they want to keep up with inflation. Only tax-free investors such as pension funds and charitable institutions can use cash equivalents to achieve a modest real return at low risk. A 12 percent nominal return equates to a positive 2 percent real return for tax-free investors if inflation is 10 percent. That same 12 percent equates to a negative real return of 4 percent for an investor in the 50 percent tax bracket (i.e., $12 \times 0.5 = 6$; $10 - 6 = 4$). Taxes apply not just to the real return on cash equivalents, but to the inflation premium as well. Since the government's tax bite transforms a modest real return into a significant negative return, the taxable investor must look elsewhere for real returns.

Holding cash equivalents for any period of time is difficult for most investors, taxable or tax-free. Often they feel that their money is not working hard enough for them unless it is in a long-term asset. Cash equivalents are dull, will never double in 6 months, are seldom the hot topic of conversation at cocktail parties, and simply lack "sex appeal."

Sexy or not, cash equivalents have their uses. Tax-free investors can use them to keep a little ahead of inflation with no risk to the nominal value of their principal. Both tax-free and taxable investors can use cash as a place to park their principal when opportunities in long-term assets are less than compelling. One of the most common mistakes in investing is the compulsion to be fully invested at all times. A better approach is the "blooper theory" of investing.

The blooper theory compares investing to a baseball game where strikes are not counted until the batter (i.e., the investor) swings. Every day the pitcher throws fast balls (e.g., real estate), curve balls (e.g., stocks and bonds), and spitballs (e.g., gold). If the batter swings and misses, the strike counts in the form of money lost. If the batter simply lets the difficult pitches go by, he loses nothing and gains the income on his cash equivalents. Sooner or later—maybe years later—the pitcher gets tired of throwing difficult pitches and tosses a blooper (i.e., great investment opportunity). That is when the patient batter steps up, swings with all his might (i.e., at last invests his cash reserves), and ideally blasts the ball over the fence (i.e., makes an extraordinary profit).

## REAL ESTATE

Real estate was the premier inflation hedge during the 1970s. Homes were transformed from comfortable places to live into highly speculative assets. Except for a pause during the 1973–1975 recession, home prices went straight up at a rate faster than inflation. By 1979 conventional wisdom suggested that real estate was the perfect inflation hedge which only goes up in price.

Loss of innocence is often more painful than loss of profits. The pain of both types of loss was inflicted on investors in real estate who believed that conventional wisdom in 1980 through 1982. Home prices failed to keep up with inflation in 1980 and 1981, and actually declined in many parts of the country in 1982. Far from being the perfect inflation, real estate was exposed as a highly imperfect one. *Despite its imperfections, real estate is still one of the best long-run hedges against inflation when purchased at a reasonable price.*

The remainder of this section treats real estate in three periods: why it was a great inflation hedge in the 1970s; why it was a disaster in 1980 through 1982; and why it should be a good investment if inflation accelerates again later in this decade.

## PERFORMANCE DURING PAST INFLATION

Inflation favors rents over profits, as property owners and shareholders discovered to their pleasure and pain, respectively, during the inflation of the 1970s. An apartment, house, or office building enjoys no productivity gains as computers do; it just sits there and provides the same level of occupancy services year after year after year. It also collects more rental income year after year, which is what a good inflation hedge is all about:

Real estate is the asset with the best natural indexation to inflation. People spend a roughly constant portion of their incomes on housing, so rents and home prices tend to go up in line with personal incomes over a long period of time. Shopping centers often fix their rents at some proportion of tenants' sales volume, so their rents rise along with the general inflation of goods and services.

Real estate uses large amounts of debt, which multiplies the return on its owners' equity. Borrowing at 8 percent to buy a property appreciating at 15 percent creates a 7 percent differential in favor of the owner. If the owner borrows 80 percent of the property's value (a debt-to-equity ratio of 4 to 1), then the return on equity amounts to 43 percent (i.e., 4 X 7 = 28; 28 + 15 = 43). Borrowers repay their debts in cheaper dollars while rising rental income pushes up the value of their properties, creating the best of all possible worlds for borrowers and the worst of all possible worlds for lenders (more about lenders later).

Real estate enjoys very favorable tax treatment. Interest on debt is tax deductible, but the profits on property are effectively tax-free as long as the owner uses the proceeds to buy another property. Income from the property can be sheltered by applying depreciation on the entire property to the income from only the owner's equity. The resulting tax shelter is often enough to cover both the owner's property income plus additional income from other sources. With a good tax accountant often there is little need to pay taxes on either income or profits from real estate.

Real estate enjoys rising margins even if rents only match the rise in the general price level. Since a large portion of property costs are fixed (e.g., mortgage payments), only variable operating costs go up. Rising rents generally are more than enough to cover those added variable costs, leaving the remainder as more profit.

Conventional accounting obscures rather than illuminates the advantages of real estate as an inflation hedge. Conventional accounting requires that income be reduced by depreciation, even if the property is well-maintained and retains its economic value. If a property increases in economic value, conventional accounting does not recognize that fact until the property is sold. Conventional accounting also requires that the inflation premium in the interest paid on debt be charged against income while ignoring the fact that the debt will be repaid in much cheaper dollars.

As an alternative to conventional accounting, real estate investors rightly emphasize cash-on-cash return. While the cash-on-cash approach has several variations (e.g., before or after principal payment on debt service), it is a more accurate way to measure the returns an investor is likely to derive from property ownership. The emphasis on cash is particularly relevant from a safety perspective since investors and corporations go broke by running out of cash rather than by running out of conventionally reported earnings.

## WHAT WENT WRONG, 1979–1982

For all its many virtues as an inflation hedge, real estate is not a perfect investment. It can become overpriced. The terms of mortgages can change. Inflation rates can change. Unfortunately for real estate investors, all those events took place at once during the 1979–1982 period.

By the fall of 1979, real estate had become vastly overpriced. Institutional investors such as pension funds bid up the prices of commercial property in their search for an asset which would outperform their plunging bond portfolios. Homeowners bid up the prices of homes to the point where few people could afford to buy their own homes at current market prices. Much of the rise in home prices came from the trend of buyers to commit ever-larger portions of their income to housing, a trend which could not go on forever.

Just as real estate became overpriced in late 1979, the Fed adopted its new policy of controlling the money supply more carefully and allowing interest rates to fluctuate, which in practice meant to fluctuate at increasingly higher levels upward. Real estate owners reacted to rising interest rates in one of two ways: the traditional strategy or the smart strategy.

The traditional strategy that homeowners employ when faced with high mortgage rates is to pull their homes off the market and wait 6 to 12 months until the Fed relents and money flows freely again. As mortgage rates rose from 12 percent to 15 percent, many homeowners pulled their homes off the market and waited patiently, but in vain. A year later mortgage rates had not declined to 12 percent, but actually had risen to over 17 percent. Not only was 17 percent a record interest rate in nominal terms, it was far above the sustained rate of increase in home prices. Slowly real estate prices began to level off and then actually declined when the homes could be sold at all. In the great national waiting contest between homeowners and mortgage rates, the clear winner was mortgage rates.

Another near winner was the homeowner who followed the smart strategy as opposed to the traditional strategy of waiting in vain for interest rates to decline. The smart strategy for a seller was to take a quick price cut to move the property. The alternative, as most traditional sellers discovered, was to sit with an unsold home and then to take a large discount later on as the price of waiting too long. The seller who took a discount quickly not only sold the home, probably at a better price than other sellers who waited longer, but enjoyed the use of the proceeds of the sale. In an age of double-digit interest rates, there is a large time value to money, and the seller who sold quickly could turn that to advantage by simply investing the proceeds of the sale in cash equivalents. The optimal strategy was to sell a home at a speculative price, enjoy money market returns on the proceeds for two years (the maximum period to avoid capital gains tax), and then purchase another home from a distressed seller at a bargain price.

Often the proceeds of the sale were not in cash, however, but rather in the form of *seller financing*. Once a rarity, seller financing became the norm by 1981, particularly in areas of heavy speculation such as California. When traditional lenders such as savings and loan associations raised their rates and shut off loans, sellers turned themselves into lenders. Seller financing has both virtues and vices, depending on whether the investor is selling or buying.

From a seller's perspective, it enables the owner to maintain the asking price, or something close to it. Many homeowners let their egos get in the way of making rational decisions about value, so seller financing makes cutting price less painful by making it less apparent. The most important rational virtue of seller financing, however, is that it may be necessary to consummate the sale. The seller's best interest is served by following three rules:

1. Get as much cash up front as possible.

2. Negotiate the best possible combination of a short-term trust deed and a rate of interest near current market rates. For many buyers the interest rate is more important than the length of the mortgage, so the best strategy may be to give a low rate of interest while keeping the maturity short (e.g., 2 to 5 years);

3. Select a buyer who appears willing and able to make the payments. When evaluating the buyer's credit, remember the three C's—character, cash flow, and collateral. The buyer's character is most important, but it may not be as verifiable as his or her cash flow and collateral.

From a buyer's perspective, seller financing offers the same prime advantage: it consummates the sale. Often, normal lenders simply close down during a period of tight money or impose mortgage terms so onerous that few buyers can qualify. Seller financing not only makes the sale possible; it also lowers the real cost of the home because it locks in a mortgage at concessionary rates. The rules for a buyer to follow are, not surprisingly, the reverse of those for the seller.

Put up as little cash as possible. In the worst case (e.g., the buyer loses his or her job and is unable to make the payments) the buyer's loss will be limited to the cash payments in most cases.

Negotiate the best possible combination of low interest rate and long mortgage term. One of the basic principles of finance is to match the maturity of assets and liabilities, which in this case means that a long-term asset such as a house should be financed with a long-term mortgage liability. The penalty for mismatching maturities was visited upon buyers who accepted 2-year second and third mortgages at 10 to 12 percent in 1980; when those mortgages came due in 1982, rates on new second and third mortgages were above 20 percent in some parts of the country.

Invest in a few hours of a good real estate lawyer's time before you put your money on the line. Many seller-financing packages involve assuming a prior second or third mortgage which may be of dubious legality. The Supreme Court upheld "due-on-sale" clauses in mortgages in 1982, a decision which created substantial uncertainty for both past and prospective buyers who assume existing low-rate mortgages. This is an occasion when a small amount of legal prevention can prevent a large amount of legal and financial pain at some later date.

The advent of seller financing reflected more than just high mortgage rates and restrictive mortgage terms imposed by traditional lenders. It reflected the demise of both the traditional lenders and their traditional 30-year mortgage.

Traditional real estate lenders, notably savings and loan associations, were crippled as a result of their past policy of mismatching assets and liabilities. They used short-term deposits to finance long-term mortgages and found themselves in a vise when short-term rates moved into double digits while their mortgages remained in single digits. Savings and loan profits turned to losses which neared a rate of $1 billion a month by early 1982. Those enormous losses forced some savings and loans into bankruptcy or merger and severely eroded the net worth of those savings and loans which remained viable. Similar but less severe losses hit other mortgage lenders such as banks and life insurance companies because they funded long-term mortgages with short-term liabilities.

The net result of all this financial carnage among traditional mortgage lenders is that they will be much more reluctant to fund another round of mortgage creation on terms favorable to borrowers. After being so badly burned, lenders will insist on variable-rate mortgages (which match their assets with their liabilities by passing the risk of changing interest rates on to the borrower) or high coupons on their fixed-rate mortgages (which impose a large cost on the borrower as compensation to the lender for mismatching the maturities of assets and liabilities).

Traditional mortgage lenders took a long time to wake up to what they did wrong. (Lenders may be slow-witted, but they are not perpetually out to lunch.) Their major mistake was to mismatch their maturities by offering 30-year fixed-rate mortgages, which they funded with short-term deposits. Their belated solution to the problem has been to switch from fixed-rate mortgages to variable-rate ones. Variable-rate mortgages come in several varieties, but their common feature is that they place the costs of inflation squarely in the lap of the borrower. The old fixed-rate mortgage was a wonderful device for passing the costs of inflation onto lenders and the benefits of inflation onto borrowers. Most of the money made in real estate in the 1970s came from fleecing lenders, but the variable-rate mortgage spoils that pleasant and profitable game. Since the interest rate on variable rate mortgages is likely to rise and fall along with inflation, "fleece the lender" is no longer an easy game to play in an inflationary world.

When trouble comes, it seldom comes alone. Trouble began when real estate became overpriced in late 1979. Trouble increased when the Fed's new policy changed the rate and availability of mortgages. Trouble multiplied further when a recessionary economy brought down the rate of inflation and brought down the appeal of inflation hedges, such as real estate, along with it.

The mortal enemy of an inflation hedge is a liquidity squeeze caused by recession and declining inflation. Recession throws investors out of work, lowers the prospective income from inflation hedges, and raises the interest rates on debt used to purchase them. Unemployed investors begin to sell their inflation hedges to maintain their standard of living, and disappointed, debt-laden investors continue selling them to prevent further losses. As the inflation hedges which investors thought could go only up go down and down, greed turns into fear and investors suffer nasty losses.

The nasty losses can be even worse if interest rates rise or remain high while inflation declines, which is what happened in 1980 through 1982. Borrowers benefit from negative real interest rates (e.g., borrowing at 8 percent to buy a home going up at 15 percent was wonderful), but they are crushed by high real interest rates (borrowing at 17 percent to buy a home going down in price was devastating through most of the 1980–1982 period). Real interest rates were high, which means trouble for borrowing-intensive assets such as real estate.

A good sign of real estate in trouble is a glut of unsold homes. Few owners are realistic enough to lower the prices of their homes fast enough to sell them quickly in a declining market. Still dreaming of the high prices of the recent past or the hopefully high prices of the near future, they hold out for a better deal while the market becomes clogged with many other homeowners doing the same thing. Whenever any kind of asset goes unsold for a long period of time, the reason is usually that its price is too high to clear the market.

It takes time for a glut of unsold property to turn into a bargain for investors. Real estate prices peaked in 1979 and began to decline in earnest in 1981 and 1982. Farmers who borrowed against the increasing value of their land found both their incomes and land values declining; Iowa farmland dropped 16 percent in price in 1982. Areas of heavy speculation such as California homes suffered even larger declines, particularly after allowing for seller financing at concessionary rates. By the fall of 1983, property prices probably will have declined far enough to make real estate a good inflation hedge again.

## REAL ESTATE AS A FUTURE
## INFLATION HEDGE

Real estate is a good inflation hedge, but not the great one it used to be. By the time conventional wisdom views real estate as a disaster area to be avoided, its price will be reasonable again. Bought at a then-reasonable price, real estate should keep up with the general course of inflation in the economy. Just keeping up with inflation may sound dull after the exciting gains of the 1970s, but that is about the best which reasonably can be expected. A major source of the past profits in real estate came from fleecing the lenders who offered long-term mortgages at rates fixed below the rising rate of inflation. Now that S&Ls and other real estate lenders have been so badly burned, they are likely to issue variable-rate mortgages which remove the property owner's ability to profit at the lender's expense on fixed-rate mortgages. Thus, rents and property prices should match inflation but not exceed it by much.

## GOLD

Gold is the world's oldest store of value. For thousands of years gold has been treasured for its luster, weight, stability, portability, and scarcity. Many civilizations on different continents in different centuries have used gold to display and store wealth.

Why gold is so compellingly attractive to so many people is a question more for historians than for economists. The paramount fact for investors is that gold is valuable because people have believed it to be valuable from the dawn of history. That belief in gold's value does not depend on a legal definition, as the belief in paper money does. It does not depend on fashion or taste, as the belief in the value of a particular kind of art does. Laws may be changed or ignored while fashions in art and collectibles come and go, but gold remains.

Throughout long periods of history, gold was the standard of domestic monetary systems. Because the quantity of gold was fairly stable over long periods of time, the price level of the nation stayed fairly stable too. Occasionally a particularly greedy ruler managed to debase the existing gold coins (one ploy was to call in all coins for exchange into new coins with the likeness of the current ruler; those new coins generally had a lower gold content than the ones they replaced), but gold usually did a good job of holding its value. Paper money was accepted only when it could be exchanged for gold; some early banks began as safekeeping warehouses for gold bullion, and their warehouse receipts functioned as paper money.

Gold also served as an international medium of exchange. Trade between nations often used gold as the means of payment. When one nation ran a balance-of-payments deficit, it lost gold. The loss of gold contracted both the nation's money supply and its economy until its demand for imports fell to its level of exports.

Gold served well as a stable store of domestic and international value by imposing a discipline on a nation's ability to expand its money supply. Popular as that discipline was with investors, it was just as unpopular with rulers and politicians who wanted *more*. The gold standard stood in their way when they wanted to enrich themselves or to buy votes from their constituents. Where there is a will there is a way, and sooner or later someone finds a way to circumvent the gold standard, inflate the currency, and create a zero sum investing game.

For all its virtues, the gold standard has a few vices too. It can be inflationary if significant new amounts of new gold are injected into the system, a situation which took place as Spain imported gold from its American colonies during the sixteenth century. The standard can be deflationary if the price of gold is set at too high a level, a disaster which afflicted Britain in the last depression. An economy growing in real terms requires a comparable increase in the money supply to keep prices constant, but there is no way for the gold standard to accommodate this reasonable need for fresh liquidity. In a time where billions of dollars are wired around the globe every day, gold seems a quaint relic of a benighted past.

"Barbarous relic" is the way most modern economists view gold. They deplore the economic waste involved in extracting gold deposits from the hole of a mine in South Africa or the Soviet Union, only to redeposit it in another hole of a bank vault located in Zurich or New York. Many economists take any serious discussion of gold as a personal affront to the progress of their chosen profession, much as a physician would take umbrage at someone who questioned the value of anesthesia or antisepsis. After all the criticism of gold has ended, there is still one intrusive fact which remains: modern economists have failed completely to provide the world with any other effective store of value.

Not that they have not tried. *Special drawing rights* (SDRs) are modern economics' contribution to rational money. Correctly noting that all forms of money (gold included) depend on a social convention to accept and use them, economists decided to create a new kind of money by creating a new convention. The International Monetary Fund was the locus of that new convention to create a new piece of paper which the world's central banks would accept as money in lieu of gold, dollars, and other reserve assets. The new piece of paper, known as an SDR (unofficially also known as paper gold) is a basket of the world's major currencies.

In theory, central banks were to use and accept paper gold. In practice, the SDR was treated as an inferior to gold when a country got into financial trouble, once again proving Gresham's law (bad money, i.e., SDRs, drives out good money). Countries experiencing balance-of-payments problems spent their currencies and SDRs first while they hoarded their gold. The Italian government even went so far as to pledge its gold as security for loans in the 1970s rather than part with its hoard of the precious yellow metal.

The yawning chasm between theory and practice creates a problem for those who would like to trust in their own government and to believe their officials. When the subject turns to gold, *governments cannot be trusted and their officials cannot be believed.* The U.S. government loudly declared that gold was obsolete during the 1960s; but when foreign central banks continued to exchange their unwanted dollars for U.S. gold, President Nixon abruptly closed the gold window to preserve the remaining U.S. hoard. Treasury secretaries during the 1970s threatened to dump the U.S. gold hoard on the market and in fact made a few small sales at low prices (alas, not at high prices), but the market called the Treasury's bluff and won. The Treasury stopped selling gold and began to act as though gold really was too valuable to let go. Such actions prove that gold really is valuable, despite the diligent efforts of public officials to convince their own citizens otherwise. Actions still speak louder than words, particularly when those words come from the public officials.

If government merely said one thing about gold while doing another, it would only confirm the existence of its own credibility gap. The problem for investors, however, is that government goes well beyond lying to its own people. Government actively tries to punish the holder of gold by making private holdings of gold illegal, by voiding private contracts calling for payment in gold, and by fixing the price of gold for long periods. The U.S. government took all three actions against investors in gold from the early 1930s to the early 1970s, and relented only under duress. When it comes to making money in gold, the unfortunate fact is that the investors' worst enemy is likely to be their own government.

After being fixed in price for 40 years, gold made up for lost time in the 1970s. Its price rose from $35 an ounce to $850 in 1980, an increase of 2328 percent. Such a phenomenal profit accrued to investors in gold who did nothing but sit on their assets, which is a major reason that the Puritan virtues of hard work, frugal saving, and productive investment are naive and quaint in a zero sum economy.

Even when gold was going up, its price demonstrated the volatility associated with all assets in a zero sum investing game. It rose sharply in the mid 1970s, as inflation increased, then declined sharply as inflation declined. It rose to new heights in the late 1970s as prices rose again and conventional wisdom suggested that double-digit inflation was a permanent fact of life. Gold's price then declined from $850 per ounce to about $300 by 1982 as the inflation rate dipped into single digits and conventional wisdom shifted from fear of inflation to fear of depression. High interest rates also pushed the price of gold down, since many investors financed their gold purchases at interest rates around 20 percent, a particularly onerous rate to pay in view of the fact that gold is a sterile asset which pays its owner *no* interest at all.

The roller coaster ride of gold prices during the last decade illustrates the volatile nature of asset prices during a zero sum investing game. Despite the fact that gold is the world's premier long-term store of value, that value is far from stable in the short run. It rises and falls by large amounts depending on economic conditions, investor concern over inflation and depression, etc. The investor looking for the ultimate asset which will remain stable in either real value or nominal price is looking for something which does not exist.

Gold is unlikely to duplicate the spectacular price rise it enjoyed during the 1970s. Much of that gain came from a catch-up after 40 years when gold's price was fixed, a condition which no longer prevails and is not likely to prevail again. In the future gold is likely to be a good *long-term* store of value, particularly when purchased at prices which have declined during the downturn of a business cycle. There is still no substitute for gold as a long-term store of value in an inflationary world, but gold is unlikely to provide large and sustained real returns in the future.

Once an investor decides to own gold, the question then arises of precisely how to do it. The best form of gold ownership is 1-ounce coins such as South African Krugerrands and Canadian maple leafs. They are convenient, portable, and easily sold into an active market. They have the additional advantage of being anonymous to the government, which cannot tax or confiscate what it cannot locate. Real estate does not have the advantage of being invisible to governments which want to extract more money from investors.

## STOCKS

Stocks seldom perform well in an inflationary world. The Dow Jones industrial average was no higher in 1982 than in 1966 despite 16 years of inflation. The reasons that stocks do poorly include the following:

Companies seldom are able to raise their reported profits as fast as general inflation in the economy, particularly if they are subject to foreign competition (e.g., steel and autos).

Reported profits can be very misleading during inflation. Depreciation is calculated on historical cost, not current replacement cost; if a factory which cost $10 million to build later costs $30 million to replace when it wears out, then the $20 million difference comes out of reported profits. If a company sells its old, low-cost inventory, then its profits may look good; but to stay in business, it must replace that inventory at current prices. If economic profit is defined as the cash left over after maintaining the basic business in good condition, then underdepreciation and inventory profits must be subtracted from reported profit to arrive at economic profit. Inflation widens the gap between economic profit and reported profit, and investors generally pay only for economic profit.

Rising interest rates during inflation reduce the present value of all future income from stocks, bonds, real estate, etc. Even if a company is able to raise its profits during inflation, rising interest rates may push down the price-earnings ratio of its stocks. Many stocks during the 1970s showed rising profits and declining P/E ratios, so their prices went nowhere on balance.

Inflation raises the value of future pension claims against a company (future retirees must be paid more), but does not automatically raise the value of pension assets. Many pension plans were heavily invested in bonds during the 1970s, so the value of their assets went down while their liabilities went up.

Despite the fact that most stocks, particularly those in capital-intensive industries, did not do well during inflation, a few stocks did. Oil stocks were sitting in the path of progress when OPEC discovered the joys of raising the price of a product with an inelastic demand curve (i.e., a product's demand curve is inelastic if large increases in price cause only a small decline in consumption). Tobacco and television broadcasting are two other examples of businesses whose revenues and discretionary cash profits went up along with inflation.

Despite the occasional exceptions, most stocks did not cope with inflation very well during the 1970s. If only because stock prices are now much lower relative to earnings and asset values than they were 15 years ago, however, stocks are likely to do better if inflation roars back later in this decade. Stocks may not do as well as gold or real estate in a future inflation, but they are likely to do better than cash and bonds.

# DIAMONDS

Diamonds did very well during the inflation of the 1970s, but diamond producers and merchants did better than diamond speculators. The investor who hopes to use diamonds as an inflation hedge must overcome several hurdles:

Transaction costs can be very high. The difference between buying and selling prices on the same stone can be as much as 50 percent, which means that very substantial appreciation is necessary merely for an investor to break even. The highest markups generally are charged by retail jewelers and high-pressure investment firms which pay large commissions to their sales staff.

Since diamonds are not uniform in size, cut, clarity, or color, even experts sometimes differ on the value of a stone. Serious investors should buy only stones certificated by the Gemological Institute of America (GIA) so that they will know their precise physical qualities. Translating constant physical qualities into current dollar quantities can be done by referring to the *Rapaport Diamond Report,* a publication which most diamond dealers have but which few are enthusiastic about showing their customers.

The future value of diamonds as an inflation hedge may be less than in their spectacular past. The zest for speculation in diamonds diminished when the price of a 1-carat D-flawless stone fell from $60,000 to $20,000 in the 1979–1982 period. (Most other diamonds fell too but by lesser amounts.) Large new supplies of stones will come from Australia and Botswana later in this decade, so rising demand for diamonds may cause an increase in the number of stones bought rather than an increase in the price of a limited number of stones.

# TANGIBLES

Some tangibles did very well during the inflationary 1970s, but predicting which ones will do well in a future inflation is nearly impossible. Like diamonds, tangible assets generally have large dealer markups. Also like diamonds, they often are nonhomogeneous, particularly paintings and other unique works. Despite these drawbacks, some tangibles have scored impressive gains during past inflations, and others are likely to do so in future ones. The record of the inflationary 1970s is illustrated

| | Compounded Annual Rates of Return* | | | | | | | |
|---|---|---|---|---|---|---|---|---|
| | 15 years | Rank | 10 years | Rank | 5 years | Rank | 1 year | Rank |
| Oil | 20.4 | 1 | 25.4 | 2 | 16.2 | 4 | --14.7 | 15 |
| U.S. coins | 17.9 | 2 | 25.7 | 1 | 13.2 | 6 | 16.8 | 5 |
| U.S. stamps | 16.8 | 3 | 19.2 | 3 | 21.8 | 1 | −6.2 | 14 |
| Gold | 16.6 | 4 | 15.5 | 5 | 17.5 | 3 | 28.6 | 4 |
| Chinese ceramics | 14.2 | 5 | 4.0 | 14 | 13.1 | 7 | 0.0 | 11 |
| Silver | 12.6 | 6 | 17.3 | 4 | 19.7 | 2 | 109.5 | 1 |
| Diamonds | 10.1 | 7 | 10.3 | 7 | 5.4 | 13 | 0.0 | 10 |
| Farmland | 10.0 | 8 | 11.7 | 6 | 7.0 | 12 | −5.7 | 13 |
| Treasury bills | 8.8 | 9 | 10.1 | 8 | 12.8 | 8 | 10.8 | 6 |
| Housing | 8.6 | 10 | 9.2 | 9 | 7.4 | 10 | 2.1 | 8 |
| Old masters | 7.8 | 11 | 8.4 | 10 | 4.1 | 14 | 1.7 | 9 |
| CPI | 7.3 | 12 | 8.5 | 11 | 9.1 | 9 | 3.9 | 7 |
| Bonds | 6.4 | 13 | 6.6 | 13 | 7.2 | 11 | 39.0 | 3 |
| Stocks | 5.7 | 14 | 7.5 | 12 | 14.8 | 5 | 51.8 | 2 |
| Foreign exchange | 3.1 | 15 | 1.4 | 15 | −2.8 | 15 | −4.3 | 12 |

* All returns are for the period ended June 1, 1983, based on latest available data; figures for the years are percents.

Source: Salomon Brothers, Inc., report, "Financial Assets—Return to Favor," New York, June 10, 1983. Table prepared by Samuel G. Liss.

in the accompanying table showing compounded annual rates of return.

# TIMING

Because asset prices are volatile in an inflationary economy, timing is a major key to profitability. Chapter 8 on fine tuning offers an approach to timing the purchase of the assets likely to benefit most in a zero sum investing game.

# CHAPTER SIX

# THE POSITIVE SUM ECONOMY

The positive sum economy is a golden age of growth, prosperity, and profit. Virtually everyone becomes better off in real terms, particularly investors who play the positive sum investing game.

## THE ECONOMIC CAUSES OF A POSITIVE SUM ECONOMY

A positive sum economy is taken for granted by most people in the last half of the twentieth century, but in fact it is discouragingly rare in history. World industrial production grew at over 6 percent in the 1949–1973 period, far higher than during any past period for which economists have firm data or are able to reconstruct it. (The next highest period of industrial growth was 4.2 percent from 1900 to 1913.) The quarter-century after World War II was a golden age of growth at rates never before attained and perhaps never to be seen again in our lifetime.

The principal cause of economic growth is deceptively obvious—people. Impressive growth has taken place in countries with vast natural resources such as the United States and in countries with virtually no resources such as Japan and Hong Kong. The countries and cultures may vary, but the common elements of people building an economy are a willingness to work, a clear connection between work and material gain, and education.

There was no doubt of willingness to work after World War II. Most people who lived through the depression believed they would have to work hard just to afford the essentials of life, to say nothing of its luxuries. The Germans and Japanese who survived the war dedicated themselves to rebuilding and redeeming their countries, in both cases with enormous success. Workaholics may not fit a psychologist's profile of a well-balanced personality, but they do generate impressive economic performance.

A willingness to work hard generally goes with a clear connection between work and material gain. American farmers are the most productive on earth because there is a direct connection between the number of bushels they produce and the number of dollars they receive. Soviet farmers demonstrate only a fraction of American productivity, partially because their socialist system cuts the connection between farm production and farm income. Developing countries often keep food prices down to subsidize their politically powerful urban populations, but that policy deprives farmers of the incentive to produce efficiently and the financial means (i.e., profits able to be reinvested in tractors and fertilizers) with which to do it. High marginal tax rates also cut the connection between more work and more income, which is why supply-side economists made tax reduction a centerpiece of their program in the early 1980s.

Money is a major incentive to work, but not the sole motive assumed by economists in their models of people as economic animals. Countries as different as Sweden, Germany, and Japan have benefited from strong social pressure to work hard. In the case of Sweden and Germany, the benefits of social pressure to work hard are diminishing as the rigorous older generation is being replaced by a soft younger one which has known only security, prosperity, and high marginal tax rates.

Education is the hallmark of a developing economy. William the Conqueror could make his mark on the world even though he could not write his own name, but little progress today is possible by illiterates. The decisive difference between developed economies and primitive ones is not how long people work (developed economies usually have shorter working hours than primitive ones, particularly when vacations and holidays are considered), but by "how smart" they work. The spread of mass education gave a massive boost to western economies during the first three-quarters of the twentieth century. Since the average level of educational attainment is leveling off, it is likely that the benefits from education are too.

Education is essential for the development and diffusion of technology, another driving force behind a positive sum economy. During this century the world has been revolutionized by electricity, telecommunications, the automobile, and air transport. Advances in medicine have added about 20 years to the average life expectancy in this century alone. Technology has been a cornucopia which promoted growth in two ways: the creation of entirely new products (e.g., television) and better methods to produce existing products (e.g., using semiconductors in place of vacuum tubes in a television set). Most of technological innovation currently in progress is the second variety which improves the quality, reliability, and cost of existing products without creating genuinely new ones.

Beneficial as it is to economic growth, technology has its problems as well. The more resources technology enables people to consume, the more the potential pollution from the by-products of those resources. Technology has created the atomic means to destroy most of the human race, a situation which has become even more of a possibility since Einstein first commented on our perfection of means and confusion of ends.

There is little such confusion over the end purpose of capital spending. The accumulation of capital enables workers to produce more goods and services and to produce them better, more safely, and with less effort. Nations with a high level of capital spending (e.g., West Germany and Japan) also often enjoy high levels of economic growth.

Growth often comes from resources as well, and in a few extreme cases resources alone suffice. The explosive growth of the oil-producing Arab states came from their good fortune to be sitting on a vast natural resource that they did not know was there, did not know how to extract, and had no use for in their primitive economies which ran on camel power. It took western companies to discover the oil, pump it out of the ground, and create markets for it in the energy-consuming developed countries. What will happen when the oil runs out is a question which bothers thoughtful Arabs, hence their investments in education, capital goods, and financial assets in the west.

The creation of markets in other countries highlights another principal cause of economic growth—free trade. World trade has expanded more rapidly than world GNP for the last generation, a trend reflected in the growth in the U.S. trade component (the average of exports and imports) of GNP from just over 4 percent in the 1950s to nearly 12 percent today. The reasons why free trade contributes to growth and efficiency were as well known to classical economists as to contemporary ones.

Free trade enables each country to specialize in producing those goods and services in which it is most efficient, and then to trade them for other goods and services produced by other low-cost countries. The net result is low cost and more efficiency for the world as a whole.

Access to foreign markets enables a manufacturer to enjoy longer production runs and lower unit costs than if producing only for a domestic market. Swiss drug companies never would have grown to a fraction of their present size if they were confined to their own tiny domestic market.

Free trade provides increased choice to consumers and increased competition to producers. When those domestic producers are inefficient or are slow to develop new products and production technologies, the threat of foreign competition can force them to catch up or go out of business. Comfortable U.S. oligopolies such as the auto and steel industries have been shaken up over the last decade by innovative and efficient foreign producers. Being shaken by foreign competition can be painful to particular inefficient producers, to their shareholders, and to their employees, but it benefits the world economy as a whole.

Growth also requires a social and political consensus to promote it, or at least not to thwart it. Growth is a messy business involving the creation of new products, many of which destroy others. If fledgling auto makers had had to pay damages to buggy whip manufacturers for the diminished sales of buggy whips, then horses still might be the prime method of personal transportation. Since growth involves the untidy upheaval of the status quo, the forces of growth and change must at least neutralize the tidy, conventional minds who compose and favor the status quo and often fight to preserve it.

The essential political condition for growth is long-term freedom for business people to act and to enjoy profits from their successful actions. Ideally that freedom comes in the context of stable politics such as the United States has enjoyed over the last century. Even when politics are as unstable as they have been in Italy since World War II, the economy still can prosper as long as business managers are sheltered from the political chaos and left free to run their own businesses. Argentina is an unfortunate example of how unstable politics disrupt the economy, keeping it well below the potential suggested by the nation's rich natural resources and educated population.

The forces fighting to maintain the political and social status quo are often secondary to the dangers of fighting a real war. European economic history over the last two centuries consists of a period of progress interrupted by a war which drowns much of the progress in blood. Once every generation or two, otherwise civilized Europeans become possessed by an uncontrollable frenzy to kill their neighbors. Except for the Civil War, the United States and Canada have been free of this periodic frenzy, so they have not suffered the destruction which attends a neighborhood war. In per capita terms the United States never has been a rapidly growing nation, but peace on the home front has enabled its modest growth rate to compound over a long period of time without wartime devastation.

Economists have given a great deal of thought to the causes of economic growth. The causes mentioned above—motivated and educated workers, technology, capital, resources, free trade, and a supportive, peaceful political system—are important, but there is something else too. At some point those forces for growth reach the point of spontaneous combustion, and everything comes together to create a dynamic economy. That dynamism is seldom the result of conscious government policies, although the Reagan administrations's supply-side economics is a conscious attempt to stimulate it. Once that dynamism is lost (e.g., postwar Britain), there are no magic formulas to restore it, and perhaps no formulas at all.

## THE FINANCIAL CAUSES OF A POSITIVE SUM ECONOMY

There is a paper economy which is very separate and distinct from the physical economy which produces and consumes goods and services. The paper economy produces and transfers paper claims on those goods and services.

When the paper economy breaks down, as it did during the 1930s, the effects can be devastating. When the paper economy works well, it promotes and facilitates real economic growth. The workings of the paper economy and its influence over the physical economy are two of the more important and lesser-understood concepts in investing.

The paper economy consists of paper claims on the physical economy's output of goods and services. Those paper claims include the standard definitions of money (i.e., cash and checking and savings accounts), commercial paper, certificates of deposit, long-term debt in the form of bonds and mortgages, insurance policies, pension rights, and common stock. Paper claims represent someone's liability to pay cash which in turn can be exchanged for goods and services.

Paper claims on goods and services can be created or destroyed. The most obvious way to create paper claims is for the federal government to print money; but they also are created by a government expanding pension rights and Social Security entitlements, by a corporation selling debt, and by a bank extending a loan to a consumer. Creating paper claims creates demand for physical goods and services except in the rare case of a liquidity trap (see Chapter 2). When paper claims on the physical economy expand faster than the physical production of goods and services, the result is likely to be inflation.

Paper claims can be destroyed as well as created, a fact which demonstrates that all paper claims are not created equal. Rising interest rates reduce the price of long-term bonds. Bankruptcies reduce the value of stocks, equity in real estate, and low-quality debt. High-quality, short-term debt is the least likely to be destroyed. Since excessive growth of the paper claims on goods and services is a major cause of inflation, a little destruction of paper claims during recession is necessary to nip inflation in the bud. Large-scale destruction of paper claims, however, results in a dramatic contraction of the demand for goods and services such as occurred in the 1930s.

The ideal is a slow and controlled creation of paper claims which creates enough demand to finance real economic growth but not enough to finance inflation. That pristine ideal is seldom realized for any extended period, but the quarter-century after World War II was as close as any in history.

The postwar positive sum economy began from a position of financial strength, which is measured in the balance sheet concepts of liquidity and solvency. The financial strength of the economy was so strong for the paradoxical reason that the depression immediately before it was so bad.

The depression of the 1930s wiped out a large portion of paper claims on the nation's goods and services. The money supply fell sharply, the stock market collapsed, companies and consumers went into bankruptcy, and debts went unpaid. The leveraged and vulnerable balance sheets of the late 1920s were wiped clean. That was little comfort to the investors whose paper claims were wiped out, but it did leave both companies and consumers in a solvent and relatively debt-free position by the start of World War II.

The depression improved solvency by wiping out debts, and then the war improved liquidity by flooding the economy with high-quality government securities. U.S. Treasury obligations were used to finance the war, and, by the time it ended, banks, companies, and individuals held large amounts of these high-quality liquid assets.

Few realized it at the time, but this combination of corporate solvency and high-quality liquidity created ideal financial conditions to begin a positive sum economy. Corporations could finance capital spending for growth by selling their U.S. Treasury securities and by borrowing against their clean balance sheets. Banks could accommodate corporate demand for loans by selling off their own U.S. government securities to obtain cash. Consumers could finance their own pent-up demand for autos, homes, etc., by selling off the savings bonds they so patriotically accumulated during the war.

The financial history of a positive sum economy is often a history of a dissipating solvency and liquidity. Banks, corporations, and individuals can finance their spending by drawing down their liquid assets and by leveraging their clean balance sheets with debt. Eventually liquid assets run dry and balance sheets become so leveraged that they cannot be leveraged any more. At that point they are vulnerable to a financial wipeout during a depression, a subject covered in Chapter 2.

If banks, corporations, and individuals all sell their Treasury securities to finance their spending, the obvious question is, who buys them? The buyer is the nation's central bank—the Federal Reserve. By trading new cash and bank deposits for privately held Treasury debt, the Fed releases liquid purchasing power into the economy to accommodate and finance its growth.

If the Fed bought only existing Treasury debt, then its ability to provide the financial means for growth would end when it had accumulated all the privately held Treasury debt in the country. In fact there is no end to the Fed's ability to accumulate Treasury debt because the Treasury usually is issuing more debt to finance federal budget deficits. When the Fed purchases newly issued Treasury securities—a process known as *monetizing the debt*—it provides even more money to finance spending in the economy.

What is virtue in moderation often is vice in excess. When the Fed monetizes a little Treasury debt, the result is to provide a moderate but ample amount of money to finance the economy's expansion. When the Fed monetizes too much Treasury debt, the result is excessive monetary creation leading to excessive demand on the economy's ability to produce goods and services, i.e., inflation.

# CORPORATE FINANCES IN A
# POSITIVE SUM ECONOMY

The previous section showed how the slow dissipation of private sector liquidity and solvency provides the financing for a growing economy. This section views the same process from the perspective of an individual company attempting to finance its growth.

The mere decision to grow looks like a radical one at the start of a positive sum game, a decision illustrated with dramatic clarity by the contrast between Sears Roebuck and Montgomery Ward. When World War II ended, Sears saw growth opportunities in retailing and built many new stores, particularly in the suburbs. Montgomery Ward's chairman, Sewell Avery, refused to expand because he believed that another depression was imminent. He kept Montgomery Ward in very strong financial condition at the cost of missing the dramatic growth opportunities which Sears enjoyed. Montgomery Ward was a financial fortress well prepared to repel an attack of depression which never came.

For companies like Sears which wanted to grow, there were four principal sources of finance to do the job: sale of liquid assets, retained earnings, sale of stock, and debt. The sale of liquid assets was covered in the previous section, and the other three methods of financing economic growth are worth separate consideration.

*Retained earnings* is the profit left after paying dividends. If a company earns 12 percent on its equity and pays out half that amount in dividends (both numbers are typical of the 1950–1973 period), then it can support 6 percent growth without increasing the ratio of debt to equity on its balance sheet. Since prices are nearly stable, that 6 percent growth represents real economic expansion.

Selling liquid assets and accumulating retained earnings are internal sources of capital which are sufficient to finance a moderately growing company, but not a dynamically growing one, for which external capital must be available on extremely favorable terms.

Debt was available to most companies at interest rates of under 5 percent, incredible as that may seem in this age of double-digit interest rates. The benefits of borrowing were enormous because the average company could earn at least twice that amount by reinvesting the money in its own business. The large positive spread between the cost of debt and the returns companies could make on it provided a comparably large incentive to use it. The result was a rising tide of borrowing to invest in new plants and equipment.

Debt is not the only source of external capital. A positive sum economy works best when equity is freely available on generous terms. "Generous terms" means that companies are able to sell large amounts stock at a premium to book value. The full implications of selling stock at a premium to book value are explored in the following chapter, but, in short, the practical result is to give companies a large incentive to sell stock and then to reinvest the proceeds in new plants and equipment. As with debt, when the incentive to sell stock is added to the availability of willing buyers of stock, the result is a flow of fresh capital to the company for use in building a new plant and buying equipment.

One sign that a positive sum game is drawing to an end is that equity capital is no longer freely available at a premium to book value. The year 1973 was picked for the end of the great postwar positive sum economy partly because that was when the stock market began to value companies at a substantial discount to replacement book value, rather than at a premium to it. (The next chapter contains additional data on replacement book value for the stock market.) This effectively closed the door of equity financing to all but a tiny minority of companies with remarkably good business prospects. Except for that tiny minority of companies (generally small technology firms), the only way for a company to secure fresh equity capital was to sabotage its own shareholders' interests by selling stock below book value.

New debt became unprofitable in the early 1980s, just as new equity became unprofitable in the early 1970s. The problem was that the return on corporate assets remained fairly static while the cost of debt soared. Borrowing at less than 5 percent was very profitable when the return on corporate assets was a bit over 10 percent, but borrowing became very unprofitable when the prime rate went over 20 percent and long-term bond rates soared into the high teens. Very few companies have safe investment projects which justify borrowing at 20 percent to finance them. Most of the companies which continued to borrow did so not because it was profitable, but because it was necessary to survive. The British, who are farther down the path to economic perdition than the Americans, have a lucid term for that practice: *distress borrowing*. Most companies can endure some period of distress borrowing, so long as that period is a short one. The decline in financial health of U.S. corporations (see Chapter 9) means that their ability to endure distress is also on the decline.

# INTERNATIONAL CAUSES OF A POSITIVE SUM ECONOMY

The international financial system is worth a separate note because of the contribution it made to the positive sum economy.

Just as World War II was ending, a small group of finance ministers met at a remote New England resort called Bretton Woods to plan the financial structure which would promote the golden age of growth over the next generation. The essence of the plan was that gold was to be the basis of world financial reserves, supplemented by a U.S. dollar fully convertible into gold between central banks (private gold ownership was still illegal for U.S. citizens). The traditional strength of gold was combined with the massive strength of the U.S. economy (in 1950 the U.S. produced half the world's GNP with only 6 percent of its population) to produce an unbeatable tower of financial strength. Britain's pound sterling also served as a reserve currency for a time, but it never was the major source of world financial strength.

The tremendous growth of trade and commerce for the next generation was financed by the release of liquidity into the world economy in the form of U.S. dollars. Marshall Plan aid, development assistance, and U.S. military spending abroad put dollars into the hands of foreigners eager to accept them. Dollars were so readily accepted because they were as good as gold, backed by the world's strongest economy, and eased the "dollar shortage" of the time. The flow of dollars stimulated and financed the world economy just as it did the U.S. economy.

The world economy also was stimulated and stabilized by two international institutions. The World Bank was created to provide advice and financing to developing nations, often on concessionary terms. The financial effect of the World Bank's loans was to provide spending power to developing countries which they in turn used to purchase goods and services from the industrialized countries.

The World Bank provided liquid purchasing power while the International Monetary Fund provided stability. When a country ran into balance-of-payments problems, generally as a result of domestic inflation, the IMF was there to provide temporary loans with stern conditions attached. Those conditions generally included currency devaluation, budget tightening, and other unpleasant steps that made nations reluctant to face the IMF. If the World Bank played the role of benevolent uncle, the IMF played the role of stern uncle.

Liquidity and solvency were the hallmarks of the financial system which emerged from Bretton Woods. Eventually the liquidity became excessive from the "dollar surplus" the United States printed to finance its war in Vietnam. Eventually the stable exchange rates broke down into floating rates in the 1970s and into competitively devalued rates (e.g., Sweden in 1982) as protectionism arose in the 1980s. Bretton Woods now is just a footnote to financial history, but while it lasted, it promoted a golden age of expansion in world trade.

## MARGINAL RETURNS VERSUS AVERAGE RETURNS

A positive sum game works best when marginal returns on capital are greater than average returns on capital.

High marginal returns give corporations a major incentive to invest in new plants and equipment. In the chemical industry up to 1970, advances in technology and increases in plant size meant that a new chemical plant had lower unit costs of production than an old one. Since lower unit costs translated into higher margins and a major advantage over the competition, chemical companies had a large incentive to grow by building large, efficient new plants.

Nowhere was the decline in unit costs more dramatic than in the computer industry. The transition from vacuum tubes to transistors and then to semiconductors lowered the unit cost of performing a computation by 99 percent in the space of a decade. New capital invested in the computer industry was matched by the large investment which actually took place and by the large profits which accrued to efficient companies such as IBM.

For most industries except computers and their microelectronic brethren, marginal returns on capital fell below average returns by 1970. In the race to lower unit costs of production, technology and economies of scale lost out to inflation. Once inflation rose to the 3 to 5 percent range, it more than offset most gains from better technology and larger plant size. By the time inflation reached double digits in the 1970s, virtually no industry except computers enjoyed higher marginal returns on capital than its average returns.

The incentive and reward for real growth are high when marginal returns on new capital are higher than the average returns on existing capital. When marginal returns on capital are well below average returns, as they are today, then real growth is the *least* profitable use a company can make of its money. Chapter 5 shows how financial cannibals capitalize on the fact that the marginal returns on capital are now well below average returns.

## THE TRIUMPH OF KEYNES

Keynes lived long enough to see his theories vindicated in practice, but not accepted by the majority of his fellow economists. His ideas reached their zenith of acceptance in the late 1960s, just as they reached their nadir of utility.

World War II solved the great problem of how to put the unemployed to work and how to get the nation's factories producing again. The federal government ran huge deficits to finance the war, and the demand those deficits created was just what the economy needed. With no significant decrease in civilian production, the nation poured forth a prodigious amount of armaments and soldiers to use them.

It would be hard to imagine a more convincing demonstration of the power of federal deficits to end depression by stimulating demand, but conventional economists of the day were not convinced. On one level they claimed that the wartime experience was unique and irrelevant to a peacetime economy. On another level, they simply were too old and too conventional to accept a new way of thinking about the economy. Their refusal to accept Keynes's theories demonstrated the typical pattern of how a new idea triumphs over old ones: it does not convince its opponents; it outlives them.

Up until the early 1960s, the Keynesians were not merely a minority; they were a youthful minority. They were young and bursting with the excitement of a radical new idea and the conviction that time was on their side. They were right. The old curmudgeons retired or died off, leaving younger Keynesians to take their places.

The young Keynesians found a willing sponsor in the young John Kennedy. Kennedy was not a brilliant economist (according to one account, the way he distinguished between fiscal and monetary policies was to remember that the letter M stood for both money and Federal Reserve chairman Martin), but he perceived a strong public demand to get the country moving again. He also recognized that conventional economists did not know how to do the job. Conventional economists had led President Eisenhower into three recessions in 8 years, and Kennedy did not want to follow that path.

Kennedy's conversion to Keynesian economics was complete when he proposed a tax cut in 1963. The economy was not in recession at the time, but a recession was forecast and Kennedy wanted to avoid it. The idea was to prevent a recession by stimulating demand through federal tax cuts. Kennedy died before the tax cut became law, but President Johnson ensured that the tax cut made it through Congress.

Recession was averted in 1964 and for the rest of the decade. Except for a brief pause in 1966, the decade was one of continuous real growth. Deficits financed both Johnson's "great society" at home and his "great war" in Vietnam. Even the most dedicated Keynesian could scarcely believe how effective deficit spending was in preventing unemployment and in stimulating the economy to ever-higher levels of production.

Acceptance by Kennedy and Johnson was a necessary condition of the triumph of Keynes's ideas. Unlike biology or physics, economics has no meaning as a laboratory science. Economics used to be called "political economy" in the recognition that political acceptance and power were essential. Without political power to translate thought into action and policy, economics is just meaningless words and sterile numbers.

Political acceptance of Keynes's ideas came from the left. Liberals wanted a more active role for the federal government in society and found in Keynes's ideas a way to justify it. Keynesians wanted political acceptance, recognition, and power, which the liberals were delighted to provide. Large federal deficits (particularly when they arose from increased spending rather than from reduced taxes) achieved both the Keynesian goal of stimulating the economy and the liberal goal of enlarging the power of government. Liberals and Keynesians enjoyed a symbiosis which led to the zenith of their mutual power in the late 1960s and which has led to a decline of their mutual power ever since.

Political acceptance started on the left and then proceeded to capture the center and part of the right as well. President Nixon was no one's idea of a liberal, but even he publicly embraced Keynes's ideas. No longer were the Keynesians young heretics battling conventional wisdom. Now the Keynesians were conventional wisdom and were proud of it.

Pride often goes before the fall, and the Keynesians were very proud just before their slow fall began. They did their best to convince the country and (which is far worse) themselves that they had banished the business cycle. They proudly proclaimed that they had cured the problem of recession and that all that was left for economists to do was a bit of "fine tuning." A few years later the finely tuned economics of the west either could not start or could not get out of first gear (see Chapter 4).

Moderate fiscal stimulus was a blessing for the economy, but moderation was not a virtue shared by Keynesians and liberal politicians. If a little pressure on the fiscal accelerator was a good thing, they reasoned, then a tromping on it with both feet would be a better one. The problem with that seductive but misguided reasoning became apparent when the economy accelerated into an uncontrolled inflation. Only when the economy was careening out of control did economists notice that the Keynesian drivers' manual pointed only to the accelerator, not to the brake. That fatal lack of symmetry plunged the economy into the inflationary 1970s.

## STABLE PRICES

Real growth and stable prices are the essence of a positive sum economy. In some cases (e.g., Brazil in the 1970s) real growth and inflation go together, but generally a positive sum economy works best when prices are stable or at least perceived to be so over the long term.

Stable prices are more than just a fetish of conservative economists. The general perception of price stability goes a long way toward defining the rules of the economic game as to how companies, investors, and workers get ahead.

When prices are stable, an aggressive company has only one avenue open to increase its sales and profits—real growth. The focus of the company's energy is likely to be on developing new products, expanding the sales and production of existing products, and reducing costs by increasing efficiency of production and marketing. All those actions contribute to a positive sum economy. As a former chairman of General Motors put it, "What is good for GM is good for the country." What is good for investors is also good for the country. The following chapter shows how investors have a strong incentive to invest in growth companies and to provide them with new equity and debt.

Ambitious and capable men and women also see their own path to riches through increasing real growth. The farmer knows that increasing his income means increasing his physical production or reducing his expenses; in an economy with stable prices, those are the only two alternatives. The worker who wants to get ahead knows that working hard to increase production is the major path to promotion. The entrepreneur who builds a company knows that the road to riches lies through more producing of goods and services.

The generation which endured the depression of the 1930s simply did not think in terms of rising prices. Their fear was deflation, not inflation. The onset of even a mild recession triggered fears of a calamity to come, so business and labor quickly became cautious about raising prices and wages. The price stability which the Keynesians took for granted in the 1960s owed much to the collective fear of depression and the inability of most people to conceive of a prolonged period of inflation. The fact that most people viewed stable prices as the norm was a major condition of a positive sum economy.

## THE HERO OF A POSITIVE SUM ECONOMY

Progress (and the lack of it) is better measured by the ideas people take for granted than by the events they actively think about and discuss.

The dominant but often unspoken assumption of the time is often the best guide to the economic and investment games in progress.

The dominant assumption of a positive sum economy is optimism. A negative sum economy begins on a note of euphoria and optimism, but ends in depression (both economic and psychological). A positive sum economy often begins with the ruins of a depression and rises like a phoenix into progress, economic growth, and the confidence that both will continue into the indefinite future.

Few people in 1950 believed they were on the verge of the greatest economic leap forward in history. Conventional wisdom feared another depression for the simple reason that depressions always followed wars (or so it was believed). The depression of the 1930s left an entire generation emotionally scarred for life. No one who had seen or, worse, experienced the bread lines and poverty of the 1930s needed convincing about the possibility of economic catastrophe.

Fear of another depression combined with the Puritan ethic to produce the dominant assumption about how a capable and ambitious person gets ahead in life—by working hard, saving money, and investing wisely. Adam Smith would have been delighted to see how the "invisible hand" dovetailed the needs of the economy with the energies of its participants. Those Puritan virtues also earned the stamp of social legitimacy for the business people and investors who created economic growth.

No such legitimacy accompanies the paths to riches during inflation or depression. The zero sum investing game is played by speculating in inflation hedges with borrowed money. The negative sum investing game is played by holding high-quality bonds. Neither of those investment strategies promotes the economic welfare of society, and both divert capable people and productive resources away from economic growth. What Adam Smith and many of his latter-day followers failed to recognize is that the invisible hand works only in a positive sum economy.

Even during the best positive sum economies, the invisible hand is imperfect in promoting the general economic welfare. A competent pickpocket who diligently pursues self-interest adds nothing to the welfare of society as a whole, but instead subtracts from it, leaving empty pockets and requiring society to fund a police and court system to deal with the pickpocket problem.

The imperfections of the invisible hand were small relative to its positive accomplishments. It channeled the energy of capable people into economic growth, stamped their activities as socially legitimate, and defined them as heroes to be emulated. The heroes of the positive sum economy are the builders: engineers, scientists, and business leaders. When the builders of society are regarded as society's heroes, then the best and brightest young men and women will be drawn to those professions. When the businessman is regarded with disdain, as he is by the upper classes in Britain, then the best and brightest will avoid productive activity like the plague. When business people are regarded with suspicion, as they were in the United States during the 1970s, then capable men and women will be drawn to professions such as law[1] which merely transfer society's wealth from one person to another without creating any more of it. The identity of society's hero is a major and often overlooked assumption which determines the economic success of a nation; in a positive sum economy the heroes are business people, engineers, and other builders of the economy.

## THE END OF A POSITIVE SUM ECONOMY

A positive sum economy can end with a bang or a whimper. It ended with a bang in 1929 and immediately became a negative sum one. It ended with a whimper in 1973 and became a zero sum economy.

Liberals took a growing economy for granted when they assumed that the relevant problem was income redistribution, not income production. Lyndon Johnson thought he could finance his "great society" programs with the surplus of a growing economy so that no one would miss the money. Later liberals assumed that they could start scores of welfare programs and provide endless entitlements with no detrimental effects on the economy's ability to expand its production of goods and services. They became so entranced with the idea of spreading golden eggs among the population that they neglected the care and feeding of the goose which laid them.

Ecologists also took a growing economy for granted when they imposed heavy burdens on business to clean up the water and air. Capital spent on cleaning up the environment was not available for increasing production. In many cases the environmental goals provided a benefit to the nation's quality of life, but they did so at the expense of the nation's ability to expand its quantity of goods and services.

The extreme version of ecology *denied* the benefits of economic growth rather than taking growth for granted. The "small is beautiful" school of economics maintained that economic growth was further un-

---

[1]Japan manages a very productive economy of over 100 million people with only 10,000 lawyers.

desirable for a host of environmental and moral reasons. The majority of humankind which wanted to improve its standard of living found this school of thought unappealing, but a number of intellectuals found it very attractive.

Every one of these trends—welfare and entitlement programs, the expansion of government power, environmental and safety regulations —sprang from good intentions. Every one of them had some good reasons for being and some good results for the country. Taken as a whole, however, these trends diverted the nation's attention and resources away from producing wealth. From an economic standpoint they were sideshows which eventually came to eclipse the main event of increasing the nation's output of goods and services.

Economists were as guilty as anyone in taking growth for granted, although they should have known better. They assumed that 3 percent productivity growth (that assumption became most firmly held just as it ceased to be true) was the normal expectation for the future so that they could devote themselves to other tasks. Keynesians in particular developed a host of methods to stimulate the demand side of the economy on the comfortable assumption that the supply side would take care of itself. When the supply side of the economy began to falter after 1973 and productivity growth slowed down, most economists were at a loss both to understand the problem and to remedy it. As physicians of the nation's economy, most economists proved incapable both of diagnosing the relevant malady and of prescribing an effective cure.

Specific signs that a positive sum game is ending include:

Capital is no longer available on attractive terms to businesses wanting to expand. Interest rates rise over the 5 percent level, reflecting either excessive real interest rates if prices are stable or rising inflation if prices are going up. Equity capital is no longer available on favorable terms when the stock market values corporate assets at a discount from their replacement value.

There are speculative excesses based on the euphoric assumption that growth will go on forever. In both 1929 and 1969, stock market speculators believed the game would never end. An economy built on speculative finance may crumble when the speculation comes to its inevitable end. Speculation may show up in leveraged and illiquid balance sheets in companies and individuals.

Public priorities shift from promoting economic growth to redistributing income, ecology, safety, etc. The general assumption that growth can be taken for granted is never true for very long.

Free trade becomes less free. Protectionism sacrifices the long-term global benefits of world trade for seldom-achieved benefits to uncompetitive workers and companies in particular nations. Since protectionism only picked up steam as the 1970s ended, it did not contribute to the end of the great positive sum investing game in 1973; the persistence of protectionism, however, will be a major force holding back the next positive sum investing game.

Fiscal policy becomes stimulative over a period of years, pointing to prolonged inflation. A contractional fiscal policy, unlikely as it currently seems, is capable of pushing the economy into depression.

Monetary policy goes off the deep end in either direction. A positive sum economy cannot survive very long in the face of a rapidly expanding or contracting money supply. A slow steady growth of the money supply is a necessary (but insufficient) condition for a healthy economy.

# CHAPTER SEVEN

# THE POSITIVE SUM INVESTING GAME

Real growth is the dominant trend of a positive sum economy, and capitalizing on that growth is the way to get rich. There are far more winners than in a zero or negative sum investing game, which makes a positive sum investing game easier and more fun to play.

## THE WINNERS—COMMON STOCKS: THE INCOME STATEMENT AND THE BALANCE SHEET

That stocks in a growing economy create wealth for their shareholders is more obvious than precisely how that wealth creation takes place.

Growth alone does not guarantee wealth to the shareholders in corporations which generate that growth. The economy grew substantially in the 16 years from 1966 to 1982, yet the Dow Jones industrial average was no higher at the end of that period than at the beginning. Creating shareholder wealth clearly involves something more than building new assets and producing more goods and services.

That something more involves two separate relationships: the cost of capital versus the returns on it and the replacement value of corporate assets versus the market value of those same assets. Those two relationships take some effort to understand, but the effort is essential to understand how wealth is created.

The relationship between the cost of capital and the returns on it is straightforward in concept. When a company can earn more on its investments than the cost of capital to make those investments, then both the company and its shareholders benefit. The positive difference between the return on capital and its cost accrues to the company as profit. Shareholders receive a double benefit, first from the profit which is attributable to their shares and second from the capitalization rate (i.e., price/earnings ratio) the stock market applies to that profit. If all this sounds a bit abstract, then the following example may make it more concrete.

There are as many different returns on capital as an accountant has fingers and toes, but the most relevant one is the return on shareholder's equity, or ROE. This is the best single measure of how well the management of a company has done in employing its capital for the benefit of the shareholders. The return on equity for U.S. industrial corporations averaged about 12 percent during most of the 1950–1970 period, with fluctuations corresponding to booms and busts of the business cycle.

The 12 percent return on equity capital is easier to measure than its cost. While finance professors go to great lengths to estimate the cost of equity capital, a reasonable and simple approach is to use the *earnings yield,* which is the reciprocal of the price/earnings ratio. A price/earnings ratio of 14, reasonably typical of the 1950–1970 period, equates to a cost of equity capital of 7 percent, simply by dividing 14 into 1.

Capital comes in two forms: equity and debt. Debt may be short-term in the form of bank loans and commercial paper or long-term in the form of bonds and mortgages. During most of the 1950–1970 period the cost of debt to good-quality borrowers was 5 percent or less. When the cost of Treasury debt rose over 5 percent in the late 1960s, conventional wisdom firmly held that such generous rates would "pull money from the moon." Because interest is tax deductible, the aftertax cost of debt was even less than its pretax cost, but, for simplicity, the following example assumes no tax effect.

If a company with a 5 percent cost of debt and a 7 percent cost of equity finances itself with equal portions of both, then its average cost of capital is 6 percent. Raising $100 million at 6 percent to invest at 12 percent gives a $6 million profit to the company after paying the cost of capital, clearly a very attractive proposition. Much of the surge in profits during the 1950–1970 period came from companies raising capital (generally debt and retained earnings) at a low cost and then investing it in plants and equipment at a much higher rate.

Companies not only reaped additional profit for themselves, but created new wealth for their shareholders. In the example above, $6 million in new profit at the company level equates to $84 million in new wealth at the shareholder level when that new profit is capitalized at a price/earnings multiple of 14 (i.e., 6 X 14 = 84). This is the essence of the wealth-creation process in a positive sum investing game. The company raises capital at a low cost, generates additional profit by investing that capital at a higher return, and then the securities market bestows wealth for the company's shareholders by capitalizing that additional profit at a generous price/earnings multiple.

This wealth-creation process depends on two critical assumptions. First, the returns on capital must be significantly higher than the cost of capital. Second, the price/earnings multiple applied to corporate profits must be reasonably constant or rising. Both those conditions prevailed during most of the 1950–1970 period, which is why it was so easy for shareholders to make money. Both assumptions, however, broke down in the 1970s. The return on capital rose only slightly during the 1970s while the cost of capital soared in response to rising inflation. A rising cost of capital meant that lower price/earnings ratios applied to a company's entire profits offset the gains which shareholders had come to expect from yearly increases in corporate profits. A more detailed explanation of why stocks did poorly in the inflationary 1970s is contained in the chapter on the zero sum investing game.

So far the wealth-creation process has been viewed from the standpoint of the income statement where a company invests its capital at a much higher rate than the capital costs. An alternative view of the wealth-creation process is to look at the balance sheet and the changes which take place there. The key to creating wealth through the balance sheet is the relationship between the replacement value of corporate assets and their market value.

The replacement cost of corporate assets means just what it sounds like: how much it would cost to buy the land, build the factories, and accumulate the inventory of a company if all those assets were replaced today. Two forces change the replacement cost of assets: productivity and inflation. Productivity drives replacement cost down (e.g., a new computer will perform as many calculations as an old one, but at half the cost) while inflation drives replacement cost up (e.g., a factory built for $10 million in 1970 probably would cost more than twice that amount to build today because of the inflation between then and now).

During a period of general price stability, productivity gains tend to lower the replacement cost of corporate assets. New plant designs, better machine tools, faster computers, and larger aircraft all combine to lower the amount of capital required to produce a unit of output. From the end of the Korean war in the early 1950s to the beginning of the Vietnamese war in the 1960s, the downward pressure of productivity gains was more than enough to offset the upward pressure of inflation. From an investor's perspective, the long-term stability of replacement costs meant that the reported book values based on historical costs in company annual reports reasonably approximated replacement book values. The inflation of the 1970s drove replacement book values far above reported book values based on historical costs of assets; however, the following example assumes they are equivalent, as they generally were in the 1950–1970 period.

Cost is one thing; market value is something else. The relationship between the replacement cost of corporate assets (represented by book value) and the market value the stock market attaches to those assets is the key to creating shareholder wealth through the balance sheet.

Growth of assets is the path to wealth when the stock market values those assets at a premium to book value. Increasing a company's assets by $1 creates more than $1 of wealth for the company's shareholders, with the precise amount of the increase in shareholder wealth depending on the size of the premium to book value represented by the price of its stock. If the stock market values corporate assets at a 50 percent premium to book value, a figure typical of the 1960s, then every $1 added to corporate assets through growth adds $1.50 to shareholder wealth. Shareholders receive a double benefit from the growth of assets, first from the increase in book value and second from the premium the stock market attaches to that book value. The larger the premium the stock market attaches to the book value of corporate assets, the larger the incentive for the company to grow and expand its assets.

The premium to book value creates ability to grow as well as the incentive to grow. If a company's investment opportunities exceed its retained earnings and borrowing capacity, then it can sell stock. The sale of stock not only provides funds the company needs for expansion; it also enhances the book value of the existing shares of stock. If a company has 5 million shares of stock with a book value of $10 per share and then sells another million shares at $15 per share, the new book value per share is $10.83. The previous shareholders thus enjoyed an 8.3 percent increase in the book value of their shares as a result of the sale of new shares at a premium to book value.

Everyone wins when the stock market values corporate assets at a premium to book value. A company has both the incentive and the financial ability to grow rapidly, something most ambitious executives enjoy doing. The existing shareholders see their wealth multiply from the growth of book value per share, the premium the stock market adds to that book value, and the opportunity to enjoy gains in book value when the company sells new stock at a premium to book value. Even the investors who purchase the new stock benefit by their inclusion in the great growth game.

Wonderful as it is, growth does not benefit shareholders in all circumstances. Growth is good for shareholders *only* when the stock market values corporate assets at a premium to the cost of replacing them. When the stock market values corporate assets at only 60 percent of the inflation-adjusted cost of replacing them, as it did in the early 1980s (see the accompanying table), then adding $1 of new assets creates only $0.60 of new wealth for the shareholders. Clearly, that is an unattractive proposition.

When the stock market values assets at a *discount* from replacement value, the policy which maximizes shareholder wealth is to forgo

| S&P 400 market trough | | Book value in year of trough | | Ratio of price to book value | |
|---|---|---|---|---|---|
| Date | Value, $ | Actual, $ | Inflation-adjusted, $ | Actual | Inflation-adjusted |
| 13 June 49 | 13.20 | 15.20 | 16.10 | 0.87 | 0.82 |
| 14 Sept. 53 | 22.70 | 20.80 | 22.70 | 1.09 | 1.00 |
| 18 Dec. 57 | 42.20 | 29.40 | 33.70 | 1.44 | 1.25 |
| 25 Oct. 60 | 55.30 | 33.70 | 38.30 | 1.64 | 1.44 |
| 7 Oct. 66 | 77.90 | 45.60 | 53.30 | 1.71 | 1.46 |
| 26 May 70 | 75.60 | 52.60 | 70.70 | 1.44 | 1.07 |
| 4 Oct. 74 | 69.50 | 67.80 | 100.70 | 1.03 | 0.69 |
| 27 Mar. 80 | 111.90 | 108.20 | 185.10 | 1.03 | 0.61 |
| | | | | 1.28* | 1.05* |
| 16 Mar. 82 | 121.20 | 118.0† | 205.0† | 1.03 | 0.59 |
| | | 127.0‡ | 225.0‡ | 0.95 | 0.54 |

| 16 Mar. 82 | 121.20 | 118.0† | 205.0† | 1.03 | 0.59 |
| | | 127.0‡ | 225.0‡ | 0.95 | 0.54 |

*Average ratio for the period.
† Estimate for 1981.
‡ Estimate for 1982.

growth in order to buy back stock. When a company can buy $1 of assets at replacement value for only $0.60 through purchasing stock, there is no incentive to build new assets. Few corporate managements are willing to forgo the expansion of their own power bases even when such stock repurchase is clearly more profitable than growth.

## THE WINNERS—COMMON STOCKS: PROFITS AND DIVIDENDS

Shareholders are the prime winners. Corporations are the prime engines of economic growth, and the benefits of that growth flow down to their shareholders in many ways.

One benefit flowing to shareholders is rising dividends, the importance of which is often underestimated. A company enjoying a sustained, rising demand for its products generally also enjoys a sustained, rising level of discretionary cash profits from which dividends can be paid.

Dividends are the basis for most (the exceptions are noted below) of the value of common stocks. Investors buy stocks because of the returns they hope to receive, and dividends constitute a major part of those returns. Most studies indicate that dividends account for a minimum of 40 percent of the total returns on common stocks over long periods of time and sometimes account for more than half.

The long-term importance of dividends is less obvious over short periods of time when the price changes in stocks are far larger than their dividend yields. Aggressive investors frequently ignore dividends in the pursuit of short-term profits, but generally that is a mistake. The long term is composed of many short terms, and after several years even the most aggressively short-term investors generally find that dividends provide a significant portion of their total returns.

Dividends are one benefit of common stock ownership; price appreciation is the other. That price appreciation is due, however, largely to rises in dividends and the popular perception that further rises will continue. Modern investment theory strongly suggests that the present value of a common stock is determined by its present and expected future dividends and by the discount rate applied to them. When a stock's price increases over a period of years, that increase generally flows from the company's increasing ability to pay dividends.

The ability to pay dividends becomes more important than the actual dividends paid once a positive sum investing game takes hold. Companies with unusually good growth prospects can pay little or no dividends to maximize their internal funds available for expansion. Investors generally believe that forgoing $1 of dividends today will result in $2 of dividends tomorrow. Most investors are willing to give up a rowboat today if they think they will be able to afford a yacht tomorrow, so stocks with low dividends and bright growth prospects are very popular.

So far the emphasis has been on dividends and the ability to pay them, rather than on reported profits. That distinction is not very important during a positive sum investing game when reported profits are a reasonably good indicator of a company's ability to pay dividends to its shareholders. That distinction becomes extremely important, however, during an inflationary economy when reported profits become distorted by underdepreciation and gains on inventory. Many companies with impressive reported profits in an inflationary economy really are going bankrupt slowly because they are starved for the cash needed to keep their plants and equipment functioning.

The spectacle of a company with reported profits slowly going bankrupt for lack of cash highlights the difference between reported profits and economic profits. Reported profits represent the accounting profession's best attempt to present the financial success or failure of a company's operations according to certain obscurely stated and loosely applied standards known as "generally accepted accounting principles." In extended periods of stable prices, reported profits do a reasonably good job of approximating the economic profit or loss incurred by a company.

Economic profits are the discretionary cash left over at the end of the year after all expenses necessary to maintain the company's business and assets in good condition. Cash is critical because only cash can be used to pay suppliers for their goods, pay employees for their services, and pay shareholders their dividends as a reward for providing the company's capital. The cash must be discretionary, rather than mandated, to pay for pollution control, to replenish the company's depleted inventory, or to restore worn-out factories because depreciation allowances are inadequate in a period of rapid inflation. Economic profits also include unrealized holding gains or losses from the ownership of assets such as land and securities, but this form of nonoperating profit is more common in periods of inflation than in periods of price stability.

## THE WINNERS—REAL ESTATE

Real estate is at its best during inflation, but it can be a winner during a positive sum investing game as well. A growing economy creates a growing demand for new buildings and a sustained demand for older ones.

The value of a property, like the value of a long-term bond, depends upon the income it generates and the discount rate applied to that income. If an apartment house can be expected to generate $1 million in income per year when it is complete and the discount rate is 8 percent, then the value of that property is $12.5 million ($1 million ÷ 0.08). If the cost to build the apartment house is $10 million, then the developer who builds it can look forward to a $2.5 million profit. In a growing economy, there are likely to be many such opportunities to pocket the developer's profit.

Owners of existing properties benefit in two ways. First, they enjoy a continuing strong demand in a strong economy, which is far better than the alternative of declining occupancy in a declining economy. Second, well-located existing properties also may benefit from rising rents even though the general price level in the economy is stable. As a growing city uses more and more land on its periphery, the rents and value of the choice land at the center are likely to go up.

Leverage magnifies the profits in real estate. If a long-term mortgage is available at 6 percent on a property which earns 8 percent, then borrowing 80 percent of the value of the property yields a current return on the owner's equity of 16 percent. If the investor is fortunate enough to see the property go up in value, then leverage magnifies the gain too. Few investments use debt as productively for the investor as does real estate in a positive sum investing game.

The three traditional determinants of real estate value—location, location, and location—are never more important than during a positive sum investing game. During a zero sum investing game, the vast majority of properties benefit from inflation, and, during a negative sum investing game, an investor is better off out of real estate altogether. A well-located property in the path of economic growth can be very rewarding, but a poorly located property may produce only indifferent returns. Selectivity is the key to good returns in real estate, which means there is no substitute for intensive homework by the investor on which property to purchase.

## THE LOSERS—BONDS AND CASH EQUIVALENTS

Cash equivalents do not lose much in nominal or real terms during a positive sum game. Treasury bills have no risk as to their nominal amount. Even other cash equivalents such as bank certificates of deposit are practically riskless, because the economy as a whole is in a low-risk mode. Cash equivalents are also riskless in real terms, because inflation is low and generally is offset by interest payments. In real terms, cash equivalents generally stay constant at worst and provide a small return at best.

Despite their lack of risk, cash equivalents are losers in a positive sum game. They lose out on the opportunity to participate in the great economic expansion going on around them. They lose the opportunity to compound their wealth in real terms. Holders of cash equivalents in a positive sum game are like the miser in the biblical tale of the talents. He buried his talent for safety rather than investing it productively so it could multiply. His miserly behavior earned him neither profits nor divine praise; he received only a well-deserved rebuke.

Bonds are likely to be worse than cash equivalents. Their nominal returns may be higher as long as the yield curve is positively sloped (i.e., long rates are higher than short rates), but their risk is much higher too. If interest rates rise for any reason, then bondholders suffer a loss of their capital. If inflation heats up, bondholders may suffer larger losses to the real value of their principal than can be offset by fixed interest payments. Long-term bonds were sold with fixed interest rates of 3 to 4 percent in the early 1950s, so the investors who bought those bonds were impaled on twin spikes of double-digit interest rates and double-digit inflation rates.

In the early 1950s the vogue was formula investing plans which shifted assets between stocks and bonds. The formulas varied, but the idea was to sell stocks after they went up and then use the proceeds to buy more bonds. By the late 1950s most of these formulas called for a maximum exposure to bonds. The investors who followed these formulas into bonds maximized their exposure to loss from rising interest and inflation rates and minimized their opportunity to participate in the great bull market in stocks.

# THE LOSERS—COLLECTIBLES

There are so many collectibles (e.g., stamps, coins, art, furniture, guns, old bottles) that useful generalization is difficult. Some collectibles may do well if they become popular with the nouveau riche created by a positive sum economy, but anticipating precisely which collectibles will benefit is a difficult game for an investor to play. The serious collector who understands a speciality well has a major advantage over the eager dilettante, but even the serious collector is handicapped by the huge transactions costs imposed by dealers, which can run as much as 50 percent of the price of the item collected. Investors are usually better off collecting what they enjoy, so that they are doubly fortunate if financial rewards are added to psychic ones.

Most collectors, serious and novice, suffer from the absence of an instant, liquid market. There is no reliable index for collectible values such as the Dow Jones industrial average for stocks. There is no liquid market for many collectibles, particularly one of a kind paintings, so an investor may not have even a remote idea of how much a collectible is worth in terms of cash.

The major problem with collectibles is that they are not the direct beneficiaries of economic growth which is the dominant trend of a positive sum investing game. The loss in collectibles is likely to be the loss of opportunity caused by tying up an investor's assets in investments where returns are likely to be lower than those available elsewhere.

## THE LOSERS—GOLD AND SILVER

The past experience of gold during a positive sum game is obscured by the fact that the price of gold was fixed at $35 per ounce from the early 1930s to the early 1970s. By fixing the price of gold for so long, the government took away the opportunity for investors to make or lose money in the yellow metal. To make doubly sure that no one would speculate in gold, the government also made the private ownership of gold illegal, except for jewelry and numismatic purposes.

Even if gold had been legal to own in a market which was free to set its price, the outcome probably would have been much the same. Inflation moves the price of gold, and there simply was not much inflation until the late 1960s. The government did investors a favor by fixing the price of gold and prohibiting its ownership, because it probably would not have been a profitable investment anyway.

Gold is the best hedge yet devised against inflation, revolution, and other chaos. Governments can't print more of it, as they print paper money. Revolutionaries can't seize it or unreasonably tax it, as they can real estate. Desirable as these qualities of gold are in some circumstances, however, they are less relevant in a positive sum game. When the name of the game is capitalizing on the real growth of the economy, gold is not where the action is.

Much the same is true of silver. It is a secondary inflation hedge, but that is not a valuable quality when inflation is a secondary concern. For both gold and silver, however, there is another factor which makes the simple inflation-hedge analysis a bit more complex.

Both gold and silver have industrial uses as well as monetary ones. Gold is used extensively in electronics for its electrical conductivity and in dentistry for its chemical stability. Silver has extensive uses in photography. In time the industrial uses of gold and silver may become more important than their monetary uses; then they may be viewed as commodities such as copper and zinc. Industrial uses are more significant for silver than for gold, but not so important as to eliminate their inflation-hedge uses.

# CHAPTER EIGHT

# FINE TUNING

The highest payoff decision an investor can make is which investment game to play. Since any single game can last up to a generation (the golden age of real growth and stable prices lasted from 1948 to 1973), an investor has plenty of time to make decisions with smaller but significant payoffs. One way to make those smaller decisions well is to use the business cycle as a timing device.

## THE BUSINESS CYCLE

The business cycle is a fixture of modern economics. Growth does not take place in a steady upward surge, but in periods of expansion followed by recessions. The average business cycle lasts about 4 years, with 3 years up and 1 year down. Not merely by coincidence, a president's term of office is 4 years too.

While every business cycle has its unique features, the general pattern coincides with a president's objectives. When a president takes office, he generally blames the current mess on his predecessor and then makes the hard decisions to clean up the mess. One of those hard decisions involves fiscal and monetary restraint to reduce inflation. While the Federal Reserve is technically independent, in practice it waits for a green light from the White House before beginning serious monetary restraint.

After fighting inflation for 1 to 2 years and blaming the accompanying recession on the last administration, a president then changes gears to ensure the reelection of his party and, last but not least, himself. A vigorous fiscal and monetary stimulus is applied to the economy so that robust growth and low unemployment are present at election time. The voters are assumed to have memories too short to remember the recession early in the president's term and brains too small to anticipate that a burst of inflation will follow the current vigorous monetary and fiscal stimulus. Generally those patronizing assumptions about the voters' memories and brains turn out to be correct.

The classic and successful example of a president who used the business cycle for his own advantage was Richard Nixon. The 1969–1970 recession reduced inflation, as did the price controls of 1971. Nixon then stimulated the economy to ensure his reelection by a massive majority in 1972 and ensure the delayed but no less direct effect of a massive burst of inflation in 1973.

Jimmy Carter did the reverse, with unpleasant consequences. Inflation was under 5 percent when Carter was elected in 1976, and might be even less today if he had spent his first 2 years fighting it as other presidents had done. Instead he stimulated the economy heavily into double-digit inflation, and only late in his term did he recognize the need to fight it. When he went into his reelection bid in 1980, he had both soaring prices and soaring unemployment to present to the voters as his economic achievements. For those and other sins, the voters returned him to the obscurity whence he came.

Political manipulation of the economy is the most easily understood cause of the business cycle, but there are other causes too. Swings in business inventories can have a large impact, particularly over 1 or 2 quarters. Swings in fixed capital spending can have an impact over longer periods. The business cycle is one of the more enduring topics of interest to economists, and they have developed a good many models to explain and predict it.

Explaining why business cycles take place is less important for investors than accepting the fact that they exist and using that fact to make money. Making money means exploiting the tendency of stocks to *anticipate* business cycle fluctuations while real estate and other assets *react* to them.

## STOCKS

Stocks anticipate the business cycle and conform reasonably well to the president's influence over the economy.

The best time to buy stock is generally late in the second year of a president's term of office. By that time his fight against inflation is vigorously under way, the economy is contracting, and no clear end to the recession is in sight. This is generally the point of maximum fear and opportunity. Stocks bottomed in the spring of 1970, the autumn of 1974, and the summer of 1982.

The best time to sell stocks is when the voters go to the polls. At that point the business cycle is in the expansion phase, corporate profits are rising, interest rates are moderate, and inflation has only begun to accelerate. The stock market generally peaks about 6 months before the economy does and is well into decline by the time recession becomes apparent.

Timing the purchase of stocks remains secondary to the decision of whether or not to buy them at all. Buying them is the right decision for a positive sum investing game and, possibly, *late* in a negative or zero sum one.

# REAL ESTATE AND TANGIBLE ASSETS

While stock prices rise and fall in anticipation of the business cycle, real estate prices rise and fall in reaction to it. That fundamental difference in the forces which move real estate prices creates a major difference in the best times to buy stocks and property.

The third year of a president's term in office is generally the best time to buy property. At that point investors are likely to have several things in their favor:

Property prices are likely to be reasonable in the wake of the recent fight against inflation, a fight which damages assets such as real estate which benefit from inflation.

Interest rates are likely to be declining, or at least are down sharply from their recent peak when the fight against inflation was being waged most vigorously.

The yield curve is likely to be positive (i.e., short-term rates are lower than long-term rates). A positive yield curve indicates a period of easy money. It also enables real estate lenders such as savings and loan associations to replenish their funds available to borrowers.

The upward surge in both inflation and real estate prices is yet to come. The economic policies which promote a happy election outcome for a president are ones which stimulate the economy and, with an increasingly small lag, inflation.

The first year of a president's term is generally the best time to sell property. At that point the seller's advantages are much the opposite of the buyer's advantages 2 years earlier:

After a period of economic expansion, incomes, inflation, and buyer confidence are all rising. The relevant concern of most investors is to find a hedge against rising prices, and real estate is one of the first inflation hedges whose price they bid up. Property prices are high because people think that the inflation of the immediate past will persist in the future.

Interest rates are likely to begin rising as the Federal Reserve shifts its policy to ensure that the inflation of the immediate past drops sharply in the future.

The yield curve begins its shift from positive to negative (i.e., short-term rates are higher than long-term ones). A negative yield curve indicates serious monetary restraint.

As with stocks, timing the purchase of real estate is secondary to the decision as to whether an investor should buy real estate at all. Real estate is a good investment in positive and zero sum investing games, but not in a negative sum one.

## BONDS AND CASH

Bonds and cash alternate in attractiveness: when one is a good investment, the other usually is not. Swings in bond prices also provide a good leading indicator for prices of other assets.

When interest rates go up, bond prices go down. Rising interest rates reduce the present value of future income, and that reduced value is transmitted instantly into lower bond prices. Rising interest rates also reduce the present value of future income from other long-term assets such as stocks and real estate, but often with a lag.

A dramatic illustration of the gap between instant and lagged response to rising interest rates took place in 1979 to 1982. When interest rates on high-quality telephone bonds rose from 12 percent to 17 percent, prices of long-term bonds fell by 30 percent. The same interest rate rise also reduced the value of homes by 30 percent, but home prices (a home's value can be viewed as a long-term stream of income in the form of rent) did not respond immediately. Intelligent sellers saw that home values were declining, quickly took small discounts to move their properties, and then invested the cash at double-digit interest rates available in short-term assets. Most sellers did not react intelligently, but, still dreaming of the prices they might have obtained in the white-hot speculative market of 1979, maintained their prices and waited for interest rates to decline. Homeowners who held out for high prices found that their homes went unsold and that moderate discounts failed to attract buyers. Unless the sellers were lucky, they eventually had to take a large discount as the cost of waiting too long. Seller financing at concessionary rates was one way for sellers to maintain both their egos and their asking prices, but that form of financing sharply reduced the real value of the transaction. It took home prices a long time to respond to high interest rates, but the response did take place and was painful to homeowners who innocently believed that home prices never go down. In many cases that loss of innocence was more painful to homeowners than the loss of profit.

Since bond prices respond instantly to rising or falling interest rates, while other assets such as real estate respond with a lag, bonds can be a leading indicator for timing the dangers and opportunities in those other assets. Timing bond prices themselves, however, is much more difficult.

Early in the second year of a president's term is when bonds are likely to be the best buy. At that point, fear of inflation is at or near its peak. Bond yields are likely to be up sharply from their previous lows, reflecting both the general fear of inflation and the Federal Reserve's tight money policy to fight it. The yield curve is likely to have been negative for long enough to make investors comfortable about holding cash equivalents and, often, even proud of holding them.

The fourth year of a president's term is generally a good time to sell bonds. At that point, investors are generally complacent because of recent good inflation numbers; only later will they become pessimistic about price stability as inflation reaccelerates. The yield curve is likely to have been positive long enough that investors have found it painful to stay in cash equivalents, so they are anxious to deploy their capital into assets with a longer maturity.

The attractiveness of short-term assets follows a cycle opposite that of bonds. Short-term assets become attractive late in a business cycle expansion (e.g., the first year of a president's term) when the Fed begins to tighten its monetary policy to fight inflation. The highest returns on short-term assets generally take place shortly after a recession has begun, but before the Fed has switched to an easy money policy to combat recession. Once the Fed switches to an easy money policy, short-term rates can decline dramatically, leaving investors who stayed short too long with a sinking feeling of lower returns and missed profits in bonds, which probably are in a bull market already.

Bonds and short-term assets are like the ebb and flow of a tide. When the tide runs in toward short-term assets, bonds are submerged by rising interest rates. When the tide goes out toward bonds, short-term assets are left high and dry. The tide generally goes in one direction for about 2 years, then reverses course.

Perhaps more than any other investments, the bonds and short-term assets changed after the Fed's new policy began in October 1979. The level of all interest rates went up, both in absolute terms and in comparison with inflation. For the first time since the 1930s, investors enjoyed a large real return on financial assets, at least on a pretax basis. In addition to raising the returns on bonds and short-term assets, the Fed's new policy raised their volatility. They are still likely to fluctuate in much the same pattern over a typical business cycle, but the fluctuations are likely to be much larger than in the quiet years before 1979.

As with other assets, timing the shifts between bonds and cash equivalents is a question which arises only when an investor has decided it's desirable to own them. For the generation up to 1979, almost every business cycle produced new peaks in bond yields and new lows in bond prices, so even an investor with great timing ability would have produced mediocre results. Bonds and cash are suitable only for a negative sum investing game.

## COMBINING LEADS AND LAGS

Since not all assets rise and fall at the same points in the business cycle, investors have an opportunity to exploit that mismatch in timing. Shifting back and forth between bonds was covered in the previous section, and a similar opportunity exists in stocks and real estate.

An investor who buys stocks in the second year of a president's term generally enjoys most of their bull market gains in the first 12 to 18 months. At that point the investor can cash in the profits at long-term capital gain rates and shift the assets into real estate which is just beginning to take off.

When real estate reaches its peak in the first year of a president's term, the investor shifts back from real estate to stocks. Since real estate is less liquid (the investor should not be too greedy and hold out too long to get top dollar for the property) than stocks, selling may take some time. The investor then sits on cash equivalents until the end of the second year of a president's term, then invests in stocks again.

Shifting back and forth between assets is never as simple in practice as it seems in theory. It involves leaving a winning asset which is still winning and moving to a losing asset which still appears to be losing.

It does not guarantee a sure purchase at the precise bottom of a market or a sale at the precise top; it merely increases the investor's chances of moving in that direction. Since all buys and sells run up the toll charge of brokerage commissions, not all the profits stay in the investor's pocket.

## CAVEATS

In the Darwinian struggle for investment survival and occasionally obscene profits, there is no magic formula which *guarantees* success. The most that investors reasonably may expect is that the knowledge and guidelines they acquire will decrease the chances of permanent loss and increase the chances of real returns.

The previous rules on timing the purchase and sale of particular assets (and indeed this entire book) are aimed at improving the odds for an investor. Even if buying stocks in the second year of a president's term, an investor may not pick the bottom for that year. In fact, it would be just plain luck if the bottom were picked. These timing rules are blunt instruments designed to help an investor recognize the periods of an asset's danger and opportunity. There are no precise instruments which enable an investor to pinpoint exact tops and bottoms in market prices.

The business cycle itself, while a regularity of our modern economy, always has a new wrinkle or two each time around. Jimmy Carter stimulated the economy during his first 2 years rather than fight inflation. Ronald Reagan went halfway during his first 2 years by simultaneously pressing on both the fiscal accelerator and the monetary brake. Candid to the core, both men clearly advertised their intentions to deviate from the norm of presidential economic practice. Other differences, often unpredictable and significant ones, will arise during future cycles, so an investor should be alert for them.

# CHAPTER NINE

# WHERE DO WE GO FROM HERE?

The previous eight chapters described the three major investing games which flow from the three major conditions of the economy. Now the obvious question is, "What is the next game likely to be, and what are the major indicators to watch?"

## THE NEGATIVE SUM ECONOMY — 30 PERCENT PROBABILITY

Seldom does a bell ring to announce the departure of one economic game and the arrival of another. Such a bell rang in October 1979 when the Fed began to fight inflation in earnest with a controlled depression.

The effects of the controlled depression are painfully apparent throughout the world:

Double-digit unemployment in many developed countries and most lesser-developed ones.

Low utilization of manufacturing capacity and low or negative corporate profits as a result.

The rise of protectionism from good intentions to preserve jobs, but with poor results for the world economy as a whole.

Extraordinarily high nominal and real rates of interest.

Declining rates of inflation, showing that depression is not all bad. Even Britain, which once seemed a permanent member of the double-digit inflation club, has reduced the rate of price increases to the moderate single-digit range.

The U.S. inflation rate for 1983 and early 1984 is likely to remain at low single-digit levels. Unemployment is still high enough to moderate wage demands, and industrial slack is large enough to restrain price increases. Productivity generally picks up at this phase of the business cycle, providing another moderating influence on unit labor costs. The lagged effects of the strong U.S. dollar in the 1982–1983 period also will help dampen inflation by providing vigorous foreign competition to domestic producers who try to raise prices. Currently high real interest rates make their contribution to price stability by motivating consumers and business people to save more and spend less (the inflationary boom of the late 1970s was largely a credit-financed one due to negative real interest rates). All this means that the short-term outlook for inflation is very positive.

Desirable as low inflation over the short term is, that is not the critical issue facing investors. The critical issue is whether inflation once again will accelerate to double-digit levels at the peak of the next business cycle (probably 1985). A review of the indicators suggests a mixed answer to that question.

The most favorable indicator is the *level of real interest rates.* As this book is written (spring 1983), all long-term interest rates are in double digits versus less than 5 percent for the latest 12-month consumer price index. Most short-term rates are in single high digits, providing positive although less substantial real rates of return. It will be difficult to stimulate another inflationary boom as long as real interest rates stay at 5 percent or more.

The *rate of money supply growth* is less encouraging. Beginning in the fall of 1982, the Federal Reserve switched from fighting inflation to fighting recession. It pushed interest rates down and money supply growth up into double digits. The Fed justified its switch to easier money on the basis of institutional factors (e.g., maturing all-savers certificates, the introduction of super NOW accounts), but the real motivation clearly was to pump up the economy. If the Fed pulls back on money supply growth by the end of 1983, then there is a reasonable chance that another burst of double-digit inflation can be avoided. If the money supply is still growing in double digits on a year-over-year basis by the beginning of 1984, then another round of inflation is highly likely.[1]

The *fiscal indicator* is the least encouraging of all. The federal deficit is currently over 5 percent of GNP and, worse, is projected by the Office of Management and Budget to remain at a high level even *after* the economy recovers from the current recession. Budget deficits at the bottom of a severe recession can provide desirable economic stimulus, but perpetual deficits mean perpetual upward pressure on aggregate demand and the price level.

The *political indicator* is mixed. The willingness to tolerate inflation is much less now than it was in the 1960s and 1970s. Unemployment at double digits, once unthinkable, became a reality in many nations in 1982 as their political leaders became more willing to inflict pain on the economy to achieve price stability. The major doubt revolves about *how long* politicians will be willing to inflict pain to drive inflation to zero and keep it there. The large and continuing budget deficits and the Fed's policy shift in October of 1982 toward stimulating the economy both suggest that there is only enough political will to keep inflation from getting terrible, but not enough political will to end it entirely.

The odds on a negative sum economy would increase in the case of a financial crisis which wipes out paper claims on goods and services. If Latin American or eastern European nations defaulted on their loans to western banks, then billions of dollars of paper claims on goods and services would be extinguished. Also extinguished would be a large portion of the equity of money center banks here and abroad, thus crippling their ability to fund another round of credit-created inflation. Crippled banks and extinguished paper claims would lower inflationary pressures, particularly if the crisis induced enough fear among consumers and business people to cause them to contract their spending and increase their saving. The pain of defaulted loans and the fear of financial crisis would not be pleasant ways to end inflation, but then, financial history is notably lacking in examples of pleasant ways to achieve price stability.

One trend which will make price stability a bit easier to attain is the diminishing power of unions here and abroad. The proportion of union-

---

[1]Currently, the best measure of money to use is M3, which is available on a timely basis and is broad enough to avoid distortion from institutional changes. The *Wall Street Journal* gives data on money supply changes frequently, or an investor can write to the Federal Reserve Board in Washington, D.C., and request its free update on the growth of the monetary aggregates.

ized workers in the labor force has been declining for years, and the power of unions in the industries they still control has declined because of the recent controlled depression, foreign competition, and deregulation in industries such as trucking and airlines. While unions are not the prime cause of inflation in the economy as a whole, they have been vigorous in pushing up wages of their members and preventing them from declining even in industries such as automobiles and steel where union wages vastly exceed world standards. The declining power of unions means that there will be fewer institutional barriers and rigidities to more flexibility and competition in setting wages.

# THE ZERO SUM INVESTING GAME—60 PERCENT PROBABILITY

Inflation need not return to double digits for the zero sum investing game to continue, although double-digit inflation is still quite possible. It is only necessary for inflation to reaccelerate from the current low single-digit level; at "only" 7 percent, inflation will demolish half of the real value of a dollar in the course of a decade.

The odds favor a conclusion that politicians really have not changed very much. Their enthusiasm for fighting inflation diminishes as the pain of unemployment and underutilized capacity mounts. At that point they switch to ensuring their own reelection by stimulating the economy. The Fed's enthusiasm for a restrictive monetary policy wanes quickly when the banks get into trouble; saving its beloved banks from the logical consequences of their own imprudent loans is a far higher priority at the Fed than fighting inflation. When the banks get into trouble, the Fed responds by shoveling money out the door.

A review of the indicators suggests why a zero sum investing game is likely to reemerge as inflation accelerates in 1984.

The fiscal indicator is strongly inflationary and is likely to stay that way even as the economy rebounds. A significant part of the "structural"[2] deficit represents the paper economy in action as the legacy of past federal generosity on Social Security and other entitlement pro-

---

[2]Politicians favor the term "structural" when they want to escape responsibility for causing or curing a problem. "Structural unemployment" and a "structural federal deficit" are phrases which absolve politicans of responsibility for building the structure or tearing it down.

grams is bestowed on the current generation of taxpapers. Promises to provide federal payments were not included in the federal budget when politicians made those promises so freely in the 1960s and 1970s, but today those past promises constitute a growing part of federal spending which is not offset by comparable growth in federal revenue.

The monetary indicator is pointed toward more inflation as this book is written in the spring of 1983. If double-digit monetary growth continues for the rest of 1983, then accelerating inflation is highly likely to rear its ugly head in 1984 or 1985. The beginning of 1984 should be an excellent vantage point to see whether the money supply (M3) is under control or out of it.

As stated in the previous section, the political indicator is mixed. There is more willingness to fight inflation than there was in past decades, but not enough determination to end inflation for good. As they have done so many times in the past, politicians are stimulating the economy thus improving both the chances of an easy election in 1984 and the chances of renewed inflation in 1985.

While a return to a zero sum economy seems most likely now, there are really two degrees of the returning inflation: moderate (high single-digit) and severe (double-digit, or "back in the soup again"). The next section outlines a scenario for a moderate zero sum economy with continued high unemployment.

## ANOTHER POSSIBLE SCENARIO FOR A ZERO SUM ECONOMY

While a return to a zero sum economy is most likely, it may be a different kind than we have experienced to date, which will combine some elements of a negative sum economy.

The business cycle, which has averaged 3 years up and 1 year down during a typical 4-year presidential term of the postwar era, may shift more toward a new normalcy consisting of perhaps 1½ to 2 years of contraction and 2 to 2½ years of expansion.

In such an economy, inflation will accelerate in the last 2 years of a president's term, but not to ever-higher levels at the peak of each business cycle. The disease of inflation will be attenuated but not permanently cured.

The cost of controlling inflation will be unemployment in high single digits and capacity utilization seldom exceeding 85 percent. Cyclical industries, which make most of their profits at the peak of a business cycle, may find the eagerly awaited peak chopped off by the early onset of the next recession. Cyclical industries with foreign competition will find profits even more elusive if the dollar remains strong and U.S. trade policy remains at least partially open.

Since fiscal policy is likely to remain stimulative because of political unwillingness to come anywhere near balancing the federal budget, monetary policy will remain reasonably tight even during a business cycle expansion. The net result is that real interest rates are likely to remain at positive levels throughout most of a 4-year presidential cycle.

Economic growth is likely to remain anemic. Like a car driven by pressing firmly on both the fiscal accelerator and monetary brake, the economy will not make much forward progress, suffering from the friction of conflicting forces.

If such a scenario materializes and inflation reaccelerates into high single digits rather than back into sustained double digits, cash equivalents should provide moderate real returns on a pretax basis over a 4-year presidential cycle. The combination of a reasonably tight monetary policy and the deregulation of interest rates should allow tax-exempt investors to maintain and moderately increase the real value of their capital. Cash equivalents are particularly appropriate for pension funds and individual retirement accounts (IRAs) of risk-averse investors who are neither willing nor able to take the chance of losing a significant portion of their capital.

Bonds are likely to provide both higher returns and higher risk than cash equivalents. Double-digit bond yields currently are higher than returns on cash equivalents because of a "fear component" concerning the chance of another burst of sustained double-digit inflation; that "fear component" will be profit to the bond investor if inflation remains even in high single digits.

Since bond prices generally are most vulnerable to tightening monetary policy in the first year of a president's term in office, an election year such as 1984 is likely to be a dangerous time to buy bonds. Chapter 10 outlines an approach to timing purchases of bonds and other assets.

Selected stocks are likely to provide positive real rates of return. High-quality companies with stable growth and moderate price/earnings ratios are likely to do best. Cyclical companies with large amounts of financial leverage and foreign competition are likely to do worst.

Real estate is likely to provide only moderate real returns plus a hedge against an unexpected explosion of inflation back into double digits. The 1979–1982 period demonstrated that property prices can go down, much to the distress of leveraged property owners who believed the myth that prices only go up. Real estate purchased in 1983 to 1984 is likely to benefit from the washout of speculation in those previous 3 years which made prices more reasonable. The potential to fleece real estate lenders, however, is far more limited than it was in the late 1970s. Instead of taking out single-digit mortgages in an era of double-digit inflation, property buyers today are taking out double-digit mortgages in an economy with low single-digit inflation. In many cases the mortgages are of the variable-rate variety which places the costs of inflation squarely in the lap of the borrower. The net result is that well-purchased property should provide only moderate real returns in an economy with single-digit inflation. If inflation roars back into double digits, however, real estate is likely to be a refuge of many investors rushing from a rotting dollar.

Like real estate, gold is unlikely to distinguish itself if the next zero sum economy is a moderate one with an acceleration of inflation only into high single digits. In that environment gold may hold its own in real terms, but its price is likely to fluctuate enough to cause discomfort to many investors seeking a stable store of value. Also like real estate, gold is likely to become far more attractive to investors if inflation soars back into sustained double digits.

Tangible assets are likely to do poorly. The dealer commissions in a round-trip purchase and sale of a tangible asset can run up to 50 percent, which means that roughly 6 years of inflation at 7 percent are necessary for an investor to merely break even. While many tangible prices declined in the 1979–1982 period, few investors really have enough expertise to know what a fair price or bargain price for any given tangible asset should be. Since positive real returns are likely to be available in financial assets, there is little incentive to accept the risks, uncertainties, and illiquid markets inherent in tangible assets.

# THE POSITIVE SUM ECONOMY— 10 PERCENT PROBABILITY

The best of all possible economic worlds is also the least likely one. A prolonged period of real economic growth is a thing of the distant past and is likely to be a thing of the distant future.

A positive sum economy is unlikely to begin until inflation is cured. Inflation simply wastes too many bright people and too many economic resources with unproductive speculation in gold, existing real estate, etc. Depression and recession, which are necessary to cure inflation, simply waste too many resources in the form of unemployed workers and underutilized factories. Even if inflation does not burst into double digits again in the 1980s, the widespread and justifiable suspicion that it might will necessitate federal policies which maintain higher than normal unemployment and interest rates and slack industrial capacity.

The expanding federal deficit also poses a barrier to noninflationary real growth. Currently the federal deficit absorbs over two-thirds of the nation's personal savings, which otherwise could be channeled into productive investments to support real economic growth. If the Fed maintains a restrictive policy and refuses to monetize the deficit (i.e., print more money), then public borrowing will crowd out private investment, leaving high interest rates and insipid economic growth as the costs of maintaining stable prices. If the Fed prints money to finance the deficit, then the normal consequence is another burst of inflation. Unfortunately there is a notable lack of a stable middle ground where printing a little more money generates a lot more noninflationary real growth.

A positive sum economy requires a general trust in the value of the dollar. That trust does not come from a single, controlled depression such as the one which ended in December 1982, but from long-term public policies to ensure stable prices. The force necessary to stop inflation roughly corresponds to the force which set it in motion. Since it took more than a decade to get inflation going, it is likely to take a comparable period before the phrase "sound as a dollar" means something more than a wasting and terminal disease.

A positive sum economy is most likely to begin from a position of financial strength, but the financial condition of the major economic players is much worse now than at the start of the last positive sum economy. Nonfinancial corporations had liquid and lightly leveraged balance sheets in 1950; today they are illiquid and heavily leveraged, as shown in the accompanying table. Banks were heavily capitalized bastions of financial strength filled with assets in the form of high-

Pretax Interest Coverage of U.S. Nonfinancial Companies (year and percent)

| 1946 | 42.9 | 1955 | 28.6 | 1964 | 11.3 | 1973 | 4.8 |
|------|------|------|------|------|------|------|-----|
| 1947 | 35.8 | 1956 | 23.3 | 1965 | 11.6 | 1974 | 4.3 |
| 1948 | 39.4 | 1957 | 15.8 | 1966 | 9.5  | 1975 | 5.2 |
| 1949 | 25.3 | 1958 | 15.0 | 1967 | 8.5  | 1976 | 6.6 |
| 1950 | 53.9 | 1959 | 13.0 | 1968 | 7.7  | 1977 | 6.5 |
| 1951 | 34.5 | 1980 | 10.6 | 1969 | 5.5  | 1978 | 6.0 |
| 1952 | 28.7 | 1981 | 11.7 | 1970 | 4.0  | 1979 | 4.8 |
| 1953 | 20.5 | 1962 | 10.4 | 1971 | 4.7  | 1980 | 4.2 |
| 1954 | 21.8 | 1963 | 11.3 | 1972 | 5.1  | 1981 | 3.5 |

*Source:* U.S. Department of Commerce data compiled in Kidder, Peabody & Co. report, *Current Investment Policy and Strategy Implementation*, April 1982, Table 5.

quality U.S. Treasury obligations; today money center banks are thinly capitalized institutions with their assets at risk from Poland to Patagonia. Consumers also have let their financial position run down over the last 30 years, but not to the degree that banks and nonfinancial corporations have done.

A positive sum economy is most likely under conditions of expanding world trade, but protectionism is the dominant economic force today. The foreign trade component (i.e., the average of exports and imports) of U.S. GNP rose from 4 percent to 12 percent over the last 30 years, which is a trend more likely to be reversed than continued. In both Europe and the United States, the concentrated pressure to save jobs in particular sunset industries such as steel and autos is gaining ascendancy over the general interest that the entire nation has in access to the best and cheapest products available anywhere in the world. When U.S. power made the rules of international commerce at the beginning of the last positive sum economy, one of those rules was that other nations should open themselves to free trade. Today the United States has little power to force other nations to liberalize their trade policies and even less inclination to avoid imposing "voluntary quotas" and other protectionist policies.

Not all the barriers to a vigorous positive sum economy are economic and financial. There is a notable lack of new inventions of the sort which transform an economy for decades. The automobile not only created a whole new industry in Detroit, but reshaped the economy by paving the nation with roads, dotting it with gas stations, and employing over 10 percent of the nation's labor force in providing goods and services to keep 100 million cars running. The telephone, the electric light, and the airplane are other now-mature technologies which created a burning need in consumers to possess them and then created the economic need for a great deal of capital investment and employment.

No comparable products to stimulate the economy are obvious today. The major force for technological change now lies in the rapidly increasing power of the computer, which largely serves to improve productivity in providing existing goods (e.g., computer-controlled robots improve manufacturing efficiency) and services (e.g., a word processor with a small internal computer multiplies a secretary's ability to type letters). The application of the computer to telecommunications is improving both the efficiency and variety of phone services, but is unlikely to have as dramatic an impact on the economy as the original introduction of the telephone. The computer will enhance productivity for the rest of this century, but, so far, video games (the author admits to a weakness for Pac Man and Frogger) and personal computers are the only two significant products of final demand created by computers.

A large amount of modesty is necessary in predicting the economic future of advancing technology. The original marketing study of the future of computers done by IBM predicted that the total number of such machines in this country would not exceed 100. Perhaps biotechnology or some other invention will provide the impetus for a vigorous positive sum economy later in this century, but currently visible technologies do not seem to suggest more than a moderate amount of economic progress.

Moderate economic progress still would be highly desirable, particularly considering the alternative of none at all. The major barriers to sustained economic progress are financial (too many debts) and economic (the continuing need to lower inflationary expectations by lowering economic activity), not technological. In the best of all possible worlds, those financial and economic barriers could be swept away to allow our economy to grow at its technological potential. In the imperfect world we live in, however, those financial and economic barriers are highly likely to keep the economy far below its potential growth rate for a long time to come.

# CHAPTER TEN

# THE VIRTUES OF INVESTING

Virtue is more than its own reward in investing; it adds to an investor's bottom line and prevents withdrawals from it. Adopting the following virtues will not guarantee a successful result, since money management is one business without a money-back guarantee. The virtues will, however, significantly increase the odds of obtaining that successful result.

## CONTRARY THINKING

Fashion is fine for clothing, but a guarantee of loss for investing. The investor has the unpleasant choice of doing the fashionable and comfortable thing which will lose money or the uncomfortable and contrary thing which will make money.

Assets become overpriced precisely because they are popular and comfortable to own. Common stocks were very popular in 1969, just as real estate and gold were very popular in 1979. All three assets were grossly overpriced at the time because large numbers of investors bought them on the soon-to-be-mistaken belief that they could go nowhere but up.

The belief that an asset can only go up, quaint as it seems with the benefit of hindsight, was supported by plausible arguments at the time. Stocks could only go up in 1969 because corporate profits would grow forever in a Keynesian-led economy which had banished the business cycle. Gold and real estate could only go up in 1979 because they were the best inflation hedges in a world with perpetual double-digit inflation. The plausible arguments are endless, and they always sound convincing.

Often the most convincing argument is "X is going up. Buy it now before it goes higher." Jumping on the bandwagon can be irresistibly appealing when everyone else seems to be making money in the favored asset. The seldom-stated premise of bandwagon psychology is that the profitable trend of the immediate past will persist into the indefinite future, or at least far enough into the future for the investors and their friends to retire rich.

In practice, it seldom works that way. Investment trends often persist longer than is rationally justifiable, but they never persist indefinitely. Trends change, often abruptly, causing great pain to investors with linear minds who assume that the future will duplicate the past. There is no scientific way to predict when an overvalued asset will begin to fall like a rock, but the long-term odds strongly favor an investor who avoids investing in the asset which is most popular in cocktail party conversations.

The cocktail party test is an unscientific but useful test of conventional wisdom. If everyone is saying, "I just made a mint in stocks (or real estate, gold coins, Tiffany lampshades, etc.)," then the favored asset is probably near its peak of popularity. If everyone thinks that any asset can only go up in the immediate future because it has only gone up in the past, then it should be sold rather than bought. Large profits are for the few, not for the many, and the sight of many people bragging about making profits in any single asset generally means that those profits are coming to an end.

The cocktail party test also illustrates why a contrary approach to investing is so hard to practice. When everyone is bragging about the money they are making in asset X, no one wants to be a wet blanket by saying that they are likely to lose their shirts and possibly the rest of their wardrobes too. That kind of public contrary opinion is more likely to make enemies than friends, even if it turns out to be true. The best investment policy is to avoid what everyone else is buying; the best social policy is to be discreet about it. Going along with the crowd is a far easier course of action; most people want to belong to the group.

In addition to the natural desire to join the group, a major obstacle to contrary thinking is lack of confidence. Deep down, many people do not have much confidence in their own opinions, particularly on a complex subject such as investing. The volatility of asset prices in recent years has given almost everyone the opportunity to be wrong some of the time, diminishing whatever confidence may have existed before. A corollary of this lack of confidence is the belief that others' opinions must be superior, regardless of whether or not they are. Lack of confidence impels investors to substitute other people's opinions for their own, often with unhappy results.

Nonprofessional investors who feel insecure when faced with the specter of competing with professionals can take a great deal of comfort from knowing that the professionals are usually wrong too. Mutual fund managers have a remarkably good record of raising cash at market bottoms and then investing it at market tops. Pension fund managers have a similarly poor record, best illustrated by the lunacy of 1971 to 1973. They invested over 100 percent of their net cash flow in stocks (the excess over 100 percent came from reducing cash and liquidating bonds), which left them very exposed to the disastrous bear market of 1973 to 1974. Worse yet, the stocks they bought heavily were the "nifty fifty," a few large-growth companies (e.g., IBM, Pfizer, Polaroid, Avon, and McDonald's) whose price/earnings multiples were raised to 60 to 70X; a few years later many of those multiples were less than 10X and many of the losses exceeded 75 percent.

Professional investment analysts have a similarly dismal track record. Surveys of the top-rated analysts' favorite stocks show an uncommonly good tendency to reflect those stocks which have done well over the last year. Not surprisingly, those same favorites also show an uncommonly good tendency to produce dismal results in the following year. Professional investors also are afflicted with the malady of projecting the profitable trend of the immediate past into the indefinite future, with the same results which insecure nonprofessionals experience.

Too much confidence can be as dangerous as too little. Just as an insecure investor is prone to rely on consensus thinking, an overconfident investor is liable to think he can do no wrong after a period of unusually good profits. The euphoric feeling that "I have this investing game down pat" generally occurs to novices who have no personal experience of being wrong but are about to have one. Investing can be a humbling experience for an overconfident investor since everyone is wrong occasionally over a long period of time. The investor who runs a little scared and is prepared to question assumptions, recheck analyses, and recognize mistakes early is likely to fare better. In investing, as in other aspects of life, pride goeth before the fall.

Perhaps the best way to overcome the psychological obstacles to contrary investing is to recognize from the start that investing requires a different mode of thought from the mode of thought appropriate to everyday living. Being a joiner is fine when it comes to team sports, fashionable clothes, and trendy restaurants. When it comes to investing, however, the investor must remain aloof and suppress social tendencies. When it comes to making money and keeping it, the majority is always wrong.

Once investors decide on the general idea of contrary investing, they usually adopt at least one of these particular approaches:

Avoiding stocks with high P/E ratios. A high P/E ratio is a good measure of a stock's popularity, just as a low P/E ratio is a good measure of its disfavor. Bargains are more likely to be found in low P/E stocks. Since high and low are relative concepts, an investor should compare the P/E ratio of his stocks with that of the stock market as a whole. The financial sections of most large Sunday newspapers contain the P/E ratio for Standard and Poor's 500 stock index.

Recognizing that most people are playing the wrong game most of the time. When everyone is buying stocks to capitalize on noninflationary growth, then the likely denouement is a recessionary decline of growth or a takeoff of inflation. If everyone is buying gold or real estate to hedge against inflation, then inflation is probably nearing a temporary (or maybe permanent) halt. If tulip bulbs, Tiffany lampshades, or some other asset of marginal economic value is registering major financial gains, then cash is a better place to be.

Looking for bargains in keeping with the Burmese adage that a man fears the tiger which bit him last, not the tiger which will bite him next. Fear of stocks is greatest when leveraged speculators have gone to the wall in a bear market, creating a buying opportunity for an investor with both ready cash and a cool head. Fear of real estate is at its greatest after a long period of high interest rates and weak property prices, forcing leveraged speculators to throw their properties on the market at distress prices. One of the early Rothschilds said that the time to buy is when blood is running in the streets, and a modern version of that is to buy an asset when the current owners of it are drowning in red ink. What causes fear in the seller is likely to cause apprehension at a minimum in the buyer, so contrary investors should accept the fact that they will never feel completely comfortable when they make their best buys.

Selling to the optimists and buying from the pessimists. Belief that the future will be completely wonderful or completely awful leads most investors to buy at high prices and to sell at low ones. The contrary investor should be on the other side of those transactions. Reality generally falls somewhere in between the worst and best that investors imagine, so betting against either extreme is usually a good policy.

Contrary investing will not produce instant profits. Nothing will. Improving the odds in their favor is the best that investors reasonably may expect. If practiced over a long period of time, however, contrary investing will keep investors out of trouble and point them toward bargains. The long-term period is critical to success, which suggests another virtue of investing—patience.

## PATIENCE

Patience is a virtue with a strange distribution among investors. Young investors have all the time in the world to enjoy the long-term benefits of patient investing, but they generally are the least patient. They want instant gratification and immediate results. They want everything right now, including instant investment performance. Young investors who own stocks are likely to check their prices on a daily or hourly basis even when they are not actively buying and selling.

Old investors do not have much time left and are actuarially unlikely to enjoy the long-term results of patient investing. Their lives are entering their twilight years, yet they invest as if there will be an infinite number of tomorrows. Old investors tend to be patient investors despite the apparent lack of payoff from that patience.

For both young and old, temperament plays a larger role in their investing than most care to acknowledge. The young in a hurry in their business and social lives are likely to be in a hurry to see investment results too. The old who are patient in most other aspects of life are likely to be patient in investing too.

For the investors of any age who can rise above their own temperaments and choose rational courses of action which are most likely to enrich them, there are compelling arguments for choosing patience.

Patience is necessary simply by nature of the investing game itself. Over short periods of 1 to 2 years, luck is probably more important than skill. Stock prices have a large random element to them, analogous to Brownian motion in physics. That random motion of stock prices is a more important determinant of profits and losses than are skill and strategy in the short run. Only over periods of 3 to 5 years do the random movements of stock prices cancel each other out, leaving the net result of the investor's intelligence and diligence.

Luck can play a dominant role in short-term real estate results too. Perhaps a new shopping center will build adjacent to the investor's property; better yet, on the property. Perhaps a rich couple will fall in love with the house an investor is selling and will pay handsomely in order to get it. Perhaps the solid citizen to whom the investor sold a house suddenly defaults on a second trust deed, declares bankruptcy, and ties up the investor in lengthy and expensive court proceedings. Such events can have a major impact on a property owner's short-term results. But in the long run, the good luck and bad luck cancel each other out, leaving a net result which is due primarily to an investor's own efforts.

Patience focuses an investor's attention on the goal of compounding money over a long period. Compounding can be magic, even when the compounding rate is modest. Investors who compound their money in real terms at 7 percent per year will double it in 10 years; in 40 years they will have 16 times their original amount. If the Indians and their descendants who sold Manhattan for $24 had been successful in compounding their money at 7 percent after taxes for the last 350 years, they would have about $30 billion today.

That $30 billion demonstrates more than the magic of compounding at even moderate rates of return. The complete absence of any pools of private capital remotely approaching $30 billion suggests that long-term compounding is an extraordinarily difficult feat. Even if one or two generations of investors are capable enough to accumulate and compound a respectable pool of assets, one of the heirs is likely to dissipate or lose it all.

The mortal enemy of compounding is the wipeout. A respectable rate of compounding for a lifetime can be lost with a single bad investment decision. The odds are that an investor will make that decision, or one of the investor's heirs will. Reducing the odds of a wipeout and raising the rate of compounding are the twin goals of this book.

Patience has more than the long-term advantage of focusing an investor's attention on the goals of long-term compounding and avoiding a wipeout. Patience also helps control short-term brokerage costs as well. The patient investor is less likely to buy and sell often, thereby reducing the 6 percent that a real estate broker charges or the roughly 3 to 4 percent that a normal stockbroker charges for a round trip to sell one stock and buy another (discount brokers charge much less, and a stockholder should use one). A toll charge of 3 to 6 percent may seem small in relation to the total amount of an investor's principal, but it is large in relation to the annual income and profit received. If, for example, an impatient stockholder makes 10 percent per year in profits and turns over his portfolio twice a year at an average cost of 3 percent per turn, then 60 percent of his annual profits go to his broker! At the end of each year investors should add up their brokerage commissions along with their net profits, and then compare the two figures to see whether it is they or their brokers who are making the most money off the investments.

## DILIGENCE, OR KNOWLEDGE IS PROFIT

There is no point in playing an investing game without an unfair advantage. Games such as tennis and golf are structured to avoid giving an advantage to any one player, which is the way it should be to achieve a sporting competition. Unlike tennis or golf, the investing game is not played for sporting competition; it is played to make and keep money. The investor's odds of making and keeping money increase in proportion to the advantages the person can accumulate over other investors. One of the most important advantages is superior knowledge about the asset one is buying or selling.

That advantage of superior knowledge generally is obtained by diligence. In real estate that advantage is obtained by knowing more about the property than the person on the other side of the transaction. Recent sales of comparable property, zoning and assessment changes, plans for nearby developments, current financing available, and many other details go into making a knowledgeable real estate investor. That knowledge does not come easily; an investor has to work to obtain it and to keep current about it.

Superior knowledge confers a comparable advantage on a stockholder in a positive sum investing game. Stockholders who are not willing or able to work very hard to become knowledgeable about their securities are best advised to find a good mutual fund run by portfolio managers who do work hard. Stockholders who are willing to work hard should be willing to read a good many annual reports, utilize investment advisory information such as that provided by Value Line and Standard & Poor, and learn about securities research and accounting. Accounting in particular is both difficult and dry, but it is the language of finance; an investor who cannot read that language is at a significant disadvantage.

Knowledge is not only power, but profit as well. The investor's goal should be to know more about the asset being bought or sold than the investor on the other side of the transaction. This advantage of superior knowledge does not come cheaply; it takes work.

There is a temptation for intellectually brilliant people to believe that their brains can substitute for knowledge. To a degree that is true, but, often, brilliant people overestimate that degree of substitutability as well as the degree of their own brilliance. Superior knowledge almost always requires some effort.

Superior knowledge is a relative concept; adequate knowledge is an absolute one. There are many investment opportunities where no reasonable amount of research will give most investors knowledge adequate to make an intelligent decision. This is particularly true for high-technology companies whose products and processes require a level of evaluative expertise which few people possess. High technology is exciting and sexy, but also impenetrable except to investors with the specialized knowledge to understand it. A good rule of thumb: Buy only what you understand.

## VALUE ORIENTATION

Once an investor adopts a contrary, patient, and diligent approach toward finding investment opportunities, the obvious next step is to find out what those opportunities look like. Value orientation is another investment virtue which increases the investor's odds of compounding money.

Value is as protean as it is important. It comes in many forms, but its common denominator is this: Buy assets at a discount from what rational buyers are willing to pay for the entire company or property. The *private buyer rule* will help an investor avoid such manias as the "nifty fifty" stocks of 1972 and 1973 (no sane private buyer would have paid those prices) and will point toward investments which are likely to offer better returns.

Determining what private buyers are paying takes only a moderate amount of work in real estate. Benchmarks of value are common to the industry, and a little time with a good broker will produce benchmarks such as the following:

> Motels sell at three to five times gross. Since expenses generally amount to about 65 percent of gross revenues, debt service should not exceed one-third of gross. Motels can be extraordinary tax shelters, thanks to IRS regulations which allow buildings to be depreciated over 15 years and furniture and fixtures to be depreciated over 3 to 5 years.

> Apartments are priced at six to seven times gross revenues in areas where expenses are heavy and eight times gross in areas of moderate expenses. If the landlord pays tenant utility bills, then multiples of gross revenues are accordingly lower.

Condominiums in a given area may sell for $200 to $300 per square foot, with adjustments for the character of the building, height (i.e., ground floor versus penthouse), view, and physical condition.

Once a real estate investor knows the benchmarks of value for his particular interest, he is in a position to search for a property at less than its value to a private buyer. Examples of wise investment procedure include:

Looking for an apartment house with a normal return on the investor's investment, but where that return is based on below-market rents because the current owner has not been vigorous enough in raising them. The investor who buys the apartment house and then raises the rents (never a pleasant task, and occasionally an impossible one where rent control applies) will realize an immediate increase in both the rental income and the market value of the property.

Finding the "fixer-upper" which is often underpriced, whether it is an old house or an old office building. Investors generally pay a premium for the newest and the best, so older properties often generate higher returns. Fixing up an older property can add significant value over and above the costs of restoration. But an investor who takes that approach should be very careful about estimating both the time and the costs necessary for restoration. Most restoration projects come in over budget and behind schedule.

Taking the patient-vulture approach of waiting for the desperate seller. Desperate sellers usually accumulate around the bottom of a recession when they have to sell their highly leveraged properties to pay off their loans. Desperate sellers can pop up any time, however, particularly when they have moved from the area and their objective has changed from getting the best price for their home to simply getting rid of it. A good sign of a desperate seller is a property which has been on the market for some time and has taken at least one price cut. Patiently waiting like a vulture for a seller to get in trouble may sound like a hardhearted tactic, but it produces bargains.

Avoiding negative cash flow situations. Particularly near a speculative top in real estate, properties often change hands at prices so high that there is no cash return to the buyer. Buyers accept minimal or negative returns because they believe that future inflation will raise those returns to high positive levels or because they believe that a greater fool will buy the property at a greater price. Occasionally a bet on a property with a negative cash flow will be profitable, but that is a bet only for those who can afford high risks. If inflation does not raise rents fast enough, then the temporary negative cash flow becomes a permanent one; a permanent negative cash flow is a good prescription for personal bankruptcy.

A value approach to stocks is more complex than a value approach to real estate. The real estate investor buys the whole property, but the shareholder buys only a small portion. Determining value to a rational private buyer may be difficult in some cases and impossible in others. Despite the additional complexities, a value approach to stocks is much the same in purpose.

Some kinds of corporate assets sell often enough to develop benchmarks of value to a private buyer. Television stations and monopoly newspapers generally sell for 8 to 10 times their pretax profits, with stations in growth markets commanding premium prices. Oil in the ground either sells for about $10 per barrel or sells on a discounted cash flow basis using a 25 percent discount rate. Most real estate investment trusts publish the current market value of their assets in their annual reports, based on independent appraisals. Tender offers (i.e., offers by one company to buy another) also provide a good source of value to a private buyer. The investor with a good estimate of the private transactions value of a company's assets has a ceiling on what should be paid and also has a target to use in attempting to buy assets at a large discount from their fair values.

Most corporate assets do not trade often enough to establish good benchmarks of value. For large companies such as General Motors and IBM there simply is no private market. In this case investors will have to do their own valuation based on price/earnings ratios, growth rates, balance sheets, etc. (as discussed in the section on contrary thinking).

One of the most important valuation decisions is whether stocks are cheaper than bonds. Stocks were cheaper than bonds or cash equivalents for 30 years until the Fed began its new operating policy in October 1979. Since then, interest rates have gone high enough to provide real competition for equity returns. A quick test is to compare the yield to maturity on long-term treasury bonds with the earnings yield on common stocks. The financial sections of most large Sunday newspapers give the P/E ratio for the Standard and Poor's 500 stock index; dividing that ratio into 1 gives the earnings yield on stocks. Unless the earnings yield exceeds the yield *to maturity on bonds, stocks should be avoided, as shown in the accompanying table.*

Shareholders do not buy an entire company; they buy only shares in it. In practice that is a very mixed blessing. The blessing arises from the

| P/E ratio on S&P 500 | Earning yield (1/PE), % | Bond yield, % | Cheaper asset |
|---|---|---|---|
| 8 | 12.5 | 9.0 | Stocks |
| 15 | 6.7 | 9.0 | Bonds |

shareholders' passive position which enables them to receive dividends without the nuisance of running the business. (Any owner of a small apartment who has tried to evict a tenant for nonpayment of rent knows very well how much nuisance there can be in active ownership.) That passive position can be a real problem, however, when management of a company has a different set of priorities from the shareholders'. Few managements run their companies to maximize the long-term returns of their shareholders; most managements view themselves like politicians who try to please many different constituencies, and shareholders are only one constituency (others include employees, suppliers, customers, the government, etc.). Managements with this constituency approach generally aim for a satisfactory level of profits to deflect shareholder complaints, then turn to other goals. This creates only a medium-level problem for shareholders since its effect is already included in the level of profits and their growth. The real problem arises when management's interests are directly opposed to those of the shareholders; in those cases, management usually decides in its own favor. If a management team is incompetent or even senile, it is very difficult to remove and replace with a better or more vigorous management team. If the company receives a generous tender offer, management may fight tooth and nail to retain its own power and prerequisites even though the shareholders would be better off to enjoy a 50 to 80 percent premium over the market value of their stock. The separation of managers and shareholders in modern corporations drives a wedge between actual and potential profits to the shareholders. Generally that wedge is small, but in exceptional cases such as tender offers it can be very large.

Even a shareholder who buys only a tiny share of a large company should still ask the final question: Would I buy the entire company at this price if I had the means? Assuming the perspective of a long-term owner helps an investor separate the latest investment fads from solid reasons to own a business. Taking an owner's perspective helps focus an investor's attention on issues such as: Do I understand the business? Does it seem like a business with a good long-term future? What are the business risks and who are the competitors? Does the stock's price seem reasonable in relation to the value of the business and in relation to other investment opportunities?

The investor who understands the company and buys its stock at a discount from the private transactions value of its assets has gone a long way toward assuming an owner's perspective. There is a tendency for many investors, particularly institutional ones who manage pension funds and trust departments, to view a stock as just a piece of paper with a few numbers attached (e.g., P/E ratio, yield, etc.). Adopting an owner's perspective helps avoid that unfortunate tendency.

Other assets are far more difficult to value than property and stocks in terms of their worth to a private buyer. Gold is not amenable to the private buyer technique, despite its industrial uses in electronics. Commodities such as copper and silver have their primary value to industrial users for construction, power transmission, and photography, but that value varies sharply over a business cycle.

## CLEARLY DEFINED OBJECTIVES

Few investors really know their own objectives, strange as that may seem. They generally define their objectives only in fuzzy terms and then change them at the wrong time. When a bull market is near its peak, conservative investors frequently become aggressive in hope of cashing in on the bonanza. When a bear market has inflicted severe losses, aggressive investors often turn so conservative that they miss the opportunities in front of them. Investors who clearly define their objectives and stick to them stand a good chance of avoiding those mistakes.

Objectives do not start with how much money an investor hopes to make; they start with how much the investor can afford to lose. The risk an investor can afford to take depends both on finances and on temperament. A serious appraisal of finances should be a first step. How much money can be lost without severely impacting the investor's standard of living? What major expenses (e.g., a house, college tuition for a child) can be expected in the near future? A careful appraisal of income, expenses, and assets is essential to defining an investor's risk tolerance.

A careful appraisal of an investor's temperamental tolerance for risk is just as essential. There are wealthy investors who can afford large losses but who become extremely upset over even small ones. Most pension funds can afford to take a very long-term view which looks beyond the short term, but most pension fund managers are mesmerized by short-term losses. They focus on relative performance in bull markets (Is my portfolio doing better than the S&P 500?) and on absolute performance during bear markets (Am I losing any money at all?). A good test of an investor's psychological risk tolerance is to imagine losing increasing amounts of money until he gets to the point where he would wake up at night scared stiff.

An investor's risk tolerance is set by either his finances or his temperament, whichever is lower. That risk tolerance neither can nor should be defined too rigorously, but can be divided into three simple categories: low, medium, and high. Once investors begin to think in those terms, they have a useful guide as to which investments are right for them.

Writing down investment objectives is often a useful step. When a low-risk investor's friends are making a bundle of money in highly leveraged real estate, high speculative stocks, and volatile commodities, he should pull out his written objectives as a way to keep his perspective and help avoid getting caught up in the mania of the moment. When a high-risk investor sees other investors staggered by declining asset prices, he should pull out his written objectives as a reminder that now is the time to take those high risks.

Investors should not select investments *above* their risk tolerance, but frequently should select investments *below* them. Just because an investor is financially and psychologically prepared to take high risks does *not* mean that he always should have high-risk investments in his portfolio. He should take high risks only when the available opportunities pay him well to do so, and should join low-risk investors when he is not so well paid. There are times when high-risk investments become so overpriced (e.g., common stocks in 1969 and real estate in 1979) that aggressive investors are better off avoiding risks they are not well-paid to take.

## A COOL HEAD, OR FEAR AND GREED OVERCOME

"If you can keep your head when all about you are losing theirs" was one of Rudyard Kipling's required virtues for becoming a mature adult. It is also a required virtue for becoming a successful investor.

Keeping one's head is easier said than done because emotions are far more powerful motivating forces than cool, rational thoughts. The relevant emotions are greed and fear, the eternal yin and yang of investing. Understanding one's own impulse toward greed and fear, overcoming it, and then capitalizing on other investors' greed and fear are the three stages of an investor's progress.

Understanding greed and fear begins with the recognition that everyone has those two emotions. Becoming aware of those emotions, particularly when one is becoming ascendent over the other, is the first step toward overcoming them. Mark Twain once observed that "courage is resistance to fear, mastery of fear—not absence of fear." Overcoming greed and fear is something no one does completely, but some do better than others. One useful method is to maintain a certain physical and psychological distance from other investors. Greed and fear are insidiously contagious even for intelligent persons, but the degree of contagion diminishes sharply with the amount of contact with other investors who are caught in the vise of either one of those emotions.

The perspective of distance in 1929 helped a professor at Harvard Business School recognize how vastly overpriced the stock market was, a recognition which he frequently conveyed to his students. When his students graduated in June, he left his teaching post and went to Wall Street to become research director at a brokerage firm. Once immersed in the mania, he lost his perspective and allowed his greed to overcome his recognition of how overvalued the stock market was. When the stock market crashed in October, the former professor and his clients were fully invested and fully exposed to the losses which followed.

A certain distance helps prevent contagious infection by greed and fear, and so does a clear discipline. If real estate investors follow the discipline of avoiding properties with negative cash flows, they are less likely to lose their assets. If stockholders avoid stocks when bonds are cheaper, as discussed earlier in this chapter, then they are less likely to be vulnerable to bear markets. Benjamin Graham, often regarded as the father of security analysis, once observed that the discipline of a greater reliance on hard numbers and a lesser reliance on judgment (which is likely to be influenced by the emotions of greed and fear) will enhance an investor's chances of success.

Graham also had another idea with the purpose of enabling investors to capitalize on other people's greed and fear. The idea was that an investor does business with an emotionally volatile fellow named Mr. Market. At times Mr. Market is in a euphoric mood and is willing to pay large amounts of money for companies, often far larger amounts than private buyers are willing to pay. At times Mr. Market is gloomy and despondent enough to sell stocks at far less than what private buyers are paying and often at far less than Mr. Market himself bought them not long before. The investor with a cool head has an obvious advantage when he sells to Mr. Market's euphoric mood and buys from his gloomy one.

Kipling's poem goes further into the virtues of keeping a cool head:

> If you can trust yourself when all men doubt you
> But make allowance for their doubting too.

Friends, acquaintances, and coworkers probably will not appreciate a cool head who throws a wet blanket on their euphoric and greedy mania, however much a wet blanket is needed. Those same people will not appreciate a cheery, chipper person talking about the wonderful bargains available when they are gloomy and despondent over the large losses they have suffered in creating those bargains. The emotional Mr. Market is not some distant lunatic, but a cross section of the investor's friends and coworkers. If an investor wants to keep his relationships intact, he is better off keeping his own counsel about how their emotional behavior creates opportunities for cooler and more rational minds.

# MODERN PORTFOLIO THEORY

Modern portfolio theory (MPT) is a collection of ideas often used by institutional investors to intimidate their clients with jargon they can't understand and occasionally used to invest the assets of those clients. A summary of the uses and abuses of MPT follows for those readers who want to pursue this subject further.

Many individual investors may not be aware that modern portfolio theory exists, and many institutional investors wish that it didn't. While MPT is not central to winning the investment game, it does have some uses which may be surprising to curious individual investors and to their sometimes jaded institutional counterparts.

The major function of modern portfolio theory has nothing to do with managing money. Most professions, particularly law and the social sciences, develop a jargon that is impenetrable to outsiders on the general theory that outsiders will be impressed by what they can't understand. The jargon of the investment management profession is MPT. Behind the impenetrable jargon of MPT, however, there are some useful ideas for investors.

## THE JARGON

The medieval guilds regarded the public revelation of trade secrets as treachery to their profession, and today's guilds use obscure terminology to prevent that revelation. Investment management is another guild which uses thought to confuse its clients and then uses speech to conceal its thought.

Whatever its merits (or lack of them) for managing money, MPT has made a real contribution to professionalizing investment management by confusing the clients. It matters little whether bewildered clients understand the substance of terms such as "beta" and "extramarket covariance." It matters very much, however, that clients are impressed by the jargon's imposing form and that they feel awe and reverence when confronted by priestly incantations of MPT.

The contrast between form and substance is apparent by comparing physics with investment management. If Rip van Winkle were a physicist who just awoke after a sleep of 50 years, he would be amazed by new terms such as "lepton," "neutrino," and "black hole." The new terms are not just new labels posted on old concepts, but substantially new discoveries, dramatically illustrated by the discovery of how to demolish entire cities.

A physicist in a laboratory may think in terms that no human being has thought of before. This is not so for an investment manager. If Rip van Winkle were an investment manager who just awoke after a sleep of 50 years, he would be amazed by all the new terms and mathematics. On closer inspection, however, he would find that *beta* merely refers to the well-known tendency of stocks which went up together in the last bull market to decline together in the following bear market. A forbidding term like *extramarket covariance*, which refers to the tendency of similar stocks to move together, is simply a restatement of the adage that when the police raid the brothel they take the piano player along with the women. After discovering that old ideas had been reincarnated with imposing new jargon and intimidating new mathematics, he might conclude that old wine had been poured into new bottles and that nothing was really very new after all.

Unlike physics, new discoveries in investment management seldom turn out to be anything substantially new because this business always has been about risk and reward and always will be. New ways of looking at risk and reward generally turn out to be rediscoveries of old ideas. Even though the substance may not be new, however, the new jargon professionalizes investment management a la the legal profession.

Long ago the legal profession discovered that an obscure jargon intimidates clients into hiring lawyers to interpret that jargon. Today investment managers can emulate lawyers in more than conservative dress, a degree from the right school, and a soothing bedside manner. MPT gives investment managers the same kind of jargon to intimidate their clients that lawyers have. The jargon also enables investment managers to communicate with each other in terms which benighted outsiders can't comprehend, just as lawyers do.

Clarity of communication flows from clarity of thinking, but clarity in both dimensions is the mortal enemy of any professional who seeks to intimidate clients through the display of jargon and mathematics they can't comprehend. Virtually everything worth knowing in human affairs can be expressed in lucid sentences of the English language, but many professionals believe that obscurity generates more respect than clarity. For that reason there is little in the literature of MPT which qualifies under Einstein's dictum that "all things should be made as simple as possible, but not simpler."

## BETA

Beta became popular as a measure of risk after the bear market of 1969 to 1970. While beta would have been very useful if anyone used it then (virtually no one did), it has been worse than useless since.

In the late 1960s, most investors viewed risk on a stock-by-stock basis. They believed they could reduce the risk inherent in particular stocks by diversifying their portfolios. In practice, diversification often meant a collection of emerging computer companies, emerging fast-food franchise companies, and emerging conglomerates. When whole portfolios of these emerging growth companies simply submerged together in the bear market of 1969 to 1970, investors were devastated both financially and psychologically.

The psychological devastation was just as important as the financial. After years of soaring equity prices, many investors believed they were omnipotent, or at least potent enough to walk on water. The most aggressive money managers were called "gunslingers," and they went out feet first as their stocks dropped 50 to 80 percent. With both their egos and their assets devastated, investors desperately looked for some explanation as to why the disaster had taken place and some way to prevent its reoccurrence.

The explanation for the disaster lay in the concept of systematic risk. The emerging growth companies of the late 1960s may have been in different industries, but they shared two common elements: unseasoned businesses and grossly inflated stock prices. A diversified portfolio of these emerging growth companies reduced the risk of loss due to unique problems at a particular company, but it did nothing to reduce the systematic risk faced by unseasoned companies in a recession and nothing to reduce the systematic risk faced by overpriced stocks in a bear market. In their search for an objective measure of the systematic risk which had devastated them, investors focused on beta.

*Beta* is a measure of a portfolio's volatility relative to the stock market.[1] (Standard and Poor's 500 stock index usually is employed as a proxy for the stock market.) If past data shows that a portfolio rose (or fell) 15 percent when the stock market rose (or fell) 10 percent, then the portfolio has a beta of 1.5. Since the stock market has a beta of 1.0, a portfolio with a beta of less than 1.0 has less than average volatility and a portfolio with a beta of greater than 1.0 is more volatile than average. Movements of the stock market as a whole have a powerful influence on the movements of particular portfolios, and beta is an attempt to quantify that influence.

With the marvelous advantage of hindsight, investors saw that portfolios of emerging growth stocks had high betas. This implied that such portfolios would rise more than average in bull markets and decline more than average in bear markets. In fact, they did both. Leaping from reasonable explanation of the last disaster to hopeful prediction of the next one, many investors became true believers in beta as a way to identify those portfolios likely to suffer most in the next bear market.

The true believers were decimated by the bear market of 1973 to 1974. Far from identifying those portfolios most vulnerable, beta gave a false sense of security to investors whose portfolios were about to be devastated. The portfolios most vulnerable were composed of the "nifty fifty" large-growth stocks such as IBM, Merck, Avon, and Polaroid. These quality growth stocks had low betas, which suggested low risk in a bear market. They also had P/E multiples of 40 to 70X, which suggested to anyone with common sense that the stocks would be extraordinarily vulnerable to a bear market. Given a clear choice between common sense and a belief in the magic of beta, many money managers chose beta, and they saw their portfolios decline by over 50 percent as a result.

Beta clearly failed to warn investors of the relevant risk in the bear market of 1973 to 1974, but that confrontation with reality did not shake the faith of the true believers. The problem was not the idea of beta, they claimed, but merely how it was calculated. Rather than use past performance data to calculate beta, the true believers developed

---

[1]For investors with a mathematical bent, beta is the "b" term in the quadratic equation $y = a + bx$ where the $x$ axis represents the stock market and the $y$ axis represents the portfolio. Because the beta of an individual stock has only limited statistical significance, reference is made only to the beta of portfolios of stocks where the statistical significance is greater.

new and more ingenious methods (in one case known as "bionic betas"). In a remarkable display of barn door closing post horse, the true believers said the problem was not beta at all, but extramarket covariance (see the next section).

Beta proved of only limited use in the next two bear markets too. In the mini bear market of 1977, high-beta, small-capitalization stocks actually rose while the S&P 500 and Dow Jones industrial averages declined. Since large oil companies generally had moderate to low betas, their vulnerability in 1981 and 1982 to dramatic price declines was not illuminated by their betas.

Like most new ideas, beta began as heresy and ended as superstition. When it was an obscure heresy in the late 1960s, it was very useful in illuminating the major risk of the time. When beta became the established dogma in the mid 1970s, it was finished as a useful tool of risk measurement. By the early 1980s, beta was approaching the superstition phase where it generated little controversy among professional investors, only apathy.

During its established dogma phase in the mid 1970s, beta was destructive psychologically as well as financially. Most people can view the world through only one conceptual framework at a time, which is no problem when that framework is relevant to current reality. Beta was a framework relevant to the reality of 1969 and 1970, but not to the bear markets which followed. For believers in beta who found themselves and their ideas becoming less and less relevant as the 1970s turned into the 1980s, the cost to their self-confidence in many cases exceeded the cost to their portfolios. Like Keynesians in the 1970s, the true believers in beta did not enjoy the realization that they had become intellectually obsolete.

# EXTRAMARKET COVARIANCE, OR HOW GROUPS OF STOCKS MOVE TOGETHER

Stocks with similar characteristics generally rise and fall together. *Extramarket covariance* is an imposing label placed on that deceptively simple observation.

The deceptive part is in which of the many similar characteristics the stock market will choose to emphasize. Sometimes the relevant characteristic is similarity of industry (e.g., oil stocks moved up together in 1979 to 1980 and down together in 1981 to 1982). At other times size is the important variable (e.g., small-capitalization companies did better than large-capitalization ones in both the late 1960s and the late 1970s). Occasionally stocks with a combination of characteristics move together (e.g., growth stocks with small capitalizations did well in 1965 to 1968, and growth stocks with large capitalizations did well in 1971 to 1973).

Since the grouped stocks move together, it does not matter very much which particular stock in that group an investor owns. Institutional investors use this phenomenon to manage large amounts of money by trying to identify a group likely to do well and then compiling a diversified portfolio within that group. This strategy approach of trying to pick groups of winners rather than individual winners multiplies an investor's effectiveness when the investor is both right and wrong.

No amount of mathematical manipulation will identify which group of stocks with similar characteristics will be the next to rise. If the stock market suddenly decides to bless all stocks beginning with the letters A through F with a P/E multiple of 20X, there is no way to know that in advance.

Once a trend is under way, however, mathematical techniques can be helpful in identifying members of the group which have benefited from rising prices. *Covariance* is the statistical term which describes the tendency of a group of stocks to move upward (and downward) together. Nimble trend players may try to jump on the bandwagon of a group of stocks rising together, but by the time such a trend is clearly apparent, its upward momentum may be exhausted.

While only nimble trend players may use covariance to profit by identifying a rising group of stocks, even the slowest investor can use it to identify that same group before it declines. If companies A through F all rose sharply together in the last bull market, then they are likely to decline sharply together in the next bear market. Conventional wisdom and hopeful thinking will find many reasons why a few members of the favored group "should" not decline along with the rest, but such "shoulds" seldom matter much to the stock market. In a financial counterpart of Newtonian mechanics, what went up together generally comes down together.

The average investor does not have access to the computers and trained statisticians necessary to calculate covariances, but that is not as significant a disadvantage as it first appears. By the time a group of stocks has moved up together long enough to be apparent to statistical analysis, it probably also is apparent to even casual readers of the *Wall Street Journal.* Hot groups are debated, discussed, and dissected both in print and in investors' conversations. In 1969 everyone knew the hot group was emerging growth stocks. In 1973 the nifty fifty large-growth stocks were the principal topic of conversation. In 1980 the profits and stock price appreciation in oil companies were topics covered in *Time* and *Newsweek* as well as in the financial press.

Like beta, extramarket covariance is a form of systematic risk. That systematic risk may be worth the potential reward if an investor wants to make a systematic bet on a group with similar characteristics. Some of the worst losses of the last generation, however, have accrued to investors who assumed systematic risks without recognizing them until it was too late. One way to identify the systematic risk in a portfolio is by the mathematical approach used to calculate beta and extramarket covariance. Another way is the commonsense approach of asking questions: What are the similar characteristics of the stocks in my portfolio? Do my stocks seem to move up and down together? What group of stocks is currently the popular topic of conversation, and do I have any exposure to it?

# THE RANDOM WALK THROUGH
# AN EFFICIENT MARKET

Few ideas have generated more strong feelings among investors than the efficient market hypothesis (EMH), also known as the "random walk theory." Extreme proponents asserted that no one can beat the market. Extreme opponents, perceiving a challenge to their competence and their income, defensively asserted the whole business of market efficiency as nonsense. As so often happens in cases of such polarized opinion, the truth lies somewhere in the middle. The EMH can be viewed in three parts: the theory, statistical evidence for the theory, and conclusions drawn from the evidence.

The theory behind the EMH is that the stock market is a good anticipatory mechanism. The present value of a stock is the product of all currently available information about the company and the economy in which it operates. Millions of intelligent and diligent investors ensure that the stock market is efficient in processing the available information so that unusually good profit opportunities exist only for very short periods of time. When a company's circumstances change, the large number of perceptive investors quickly changes the price of the stock accordingly. In short, the stock market as a whole is more efficient in pricing stocks than any single investor.

Statistical proof of the EMH came from analyses of investment performance. Studies of stock price changes showed that past performance could not be used to predict future performance. On the contrary, stock prices showed random movements, hence the name random walk theory.

Analyses of performance by investment managers yielded similar results. Many extensive studies of the investment track records of mutual funds and other pools of money failed to yield any statistically significant evidence that anyone consistently beat the market. Most funds do well during some years, but then do poorly in others. As with individual stocks, the performance of investment managers showed a random distribution of results so that past good or bad performance did not predict future performance.

With impressive evidence that the market had been efficient, the more enthusiastic proponents advanced the strong form of the EMH which said that the stock market is so efficient that no one can beat it. More moderate proponents suggested weaker versions of the EMH to the effect that the market was difficult to beat and that there was a distinct lack of statistical evidence to back up investment managers' glowing claims of sterling performance.

Few outside the investment business can appreciate the impact of the EMH on traditional investment managers. They felt their egos and reputation threatened (in most cases deservedly so) by the assertion that they could not beat the market. Since their clients began to ask embarrassing questions, traditional investment managers perceived their own finances to be threatened, particularly since they often did not understand the statistical terms which were part of the EMH. Adding insult to injury was the fact that most of the proponents of EMH were either young and quantitatively oriented or were business school professors, and both groups were viewed with suspicion by older practicing investment managers.

The debate over EMH generated more heat than light at first, but in time the light revealed a few weaknesses of the theory. Studies done of mutual funds had a serious deficiency in that the managers of those funds often changed during the period of the study. Some later studies actually showed with statistically significant results that some managers did beat the market, but the major problem lay in the blunt nature of the statistical tools available to perform a precise task.

This book was written on the assumption that readers prefer prose to mathematics, but this is one occasion where a few numbers are necessary. Good performance by an investment manager may be defined as doing 5 percent better per year than the S&P 500. (Since 75 percent of institutional investors do *worse* than the S&P 500 over long periods of time, anyone who does 5 percent better per year on a consistent basis is doing a very good job indeed.) To be certain at the 95 percent confidence level that a manager's 5 percent margin of superior performance was due to skill rather than luck, statistical methods require 25 observations, or a quarter of a century. By the time a quarter-century has passed and statistical methods have identified a money manager as superior with a high degree of confidence, the person may have retired rich or become senile.

The reason statistical methods take such an unreasonably long time to identify a superior money manager is that the 5 percent criterion of good performance is small in relation to the 22 percent standard deviation of returns for the S&P 500. If the standard deviation were much smaller than the criterion of good performance, then the job could be done much faster. Even if there are many superior money managers out there, the statistical tools are inadequate to identify them with a high degree of confidence in time for potential clients to employ them.

The persistence of trends (see extramarket covariance) also poses a problem for the EMH. The EMH suggests a rapid market reaction to new information, not an agonizingly slow one such as the nifty fifty large-growth stocks suffered when they underperformed the S&P 500 every year from 1974 to 1980. The persistence of such trends poses a challenge to the strong version of the EMH which asserts market perfection, but not to weaker versions of the EMH which merely assert that such trends are sufficiently rare and hard to identify that few investors can capitalize on them.

As time went on, the extreme positions on both sides of the EMH began to soften. Even hardened proponents began to realize that their statistical tools were blunt and that the stock market was less than perfect at times. Even hardened opponents of the EMH began to admit that the market does a good job of evaluating available information in setting stock prices. Once the black or white views on EMH melded into shades of grey, the terms of the debate subtly changed to the degree of market efficiency. That debate over the degree of market efficiency has become the contemporary counterpart of the medieval debate over how many angels can dance on the head of a pin—a source of endless discussion without firm decision.

From the perspective of an investor who wants to make money rather than engage in endless debate, the EMH has one major lesson. Since the market does a reasonably good job of pricing stocks based on currently available information, the path to profit lies in exploiting significant information not currently available. There are three sources of significant information not available to other investors: diligence, contrary opinion, and inside information. Inside information (e.g., knowing that company A will make a tender offer for the shares of company B) is both rare and illegal to use. Diligence and contrary opinion, however, are valid methods, and they have been covered in the chapter on the virtues of investing.

# INDEX